NO BULL
~~NOBLE~~ REVIEW™

UNITED STATES HISTORY

For use with the AP® US History Exam and SAT Subject Test™

A no-nonsense approach to prepare for class and the big tests

by Jeremy Klaff & Harry Klaff

About the Authors

Harry Klaff taught high school social studies in the New York City public schools system for 34 years. In 1993, he was the honored recipient of the John Bunzel Memorial Award as NYC's social studies teacher of the year. As a member of city-wide Justice Resource Center, he helped write numerous curricula in law-related education. For many years, he created the annual Model City Council project, in which students took over New York's City Hall for a day-long simulation exercise.

Jeremy Klaff has been teaching AP History classes for over a decade. His website, www.mrklaff. com has been utilized by teachers and students across the country for review materials as well as original social studies music. Jeremy has published Document Based Questions for Binghamton University's Women's History website, womhist.binghamton.edu. He has conducted staff developments for "Entertainment in Education" at both the high school and college level. In 2006, he was included in the Who's Who of American Teachers.

Table of Contents

The No Bull Approach

Go to pg. 161 and cut out my Review Sheets. Use them to help you study.

No Bull Review…"because your review book, shouldn't need a review book!"

This review book is the most concise and to the point review available for United States History. Our goal here is to give you everything you need to know for class and standardized testing. Sometimes review books can be full of material that you just don't need to know. Or, they give explanations that are just as long as the ones found in the textbooks. The No Bull approach is to cut through the fat, and give you what you want.

We, as authors of No Bull Review, are teachers. For years, we have been speaking to students to find out what you want in a review book. The answer? No Bull. You want the facts, clear and to the point. And...you want review questions. Lots of them.

At the end of this book you will find an intense review sheet. If you know all of the terms and definitions on the *No Bull Review Sheet*, you should find success.

The practice questions in this book are our own creation, and are based on the style of questions commonly used in the curriculum. They are questions that evaluate the most important themes of United States History.

We hope you enjoy the No Bull approach. Thank you, and best of luck.

– *No Bull Review*

Colonial America, 1607-1763

The time period between 1607-1763 set the stage for United States History. People settled in the North for religious freedom. They settled in the South (Virginia) for economic opportunity. Because England only cared about their bottom line financially, they gave the colonists some social and political freedoms in what was commonly known as *salutary neglect*. The new America displayed a Great Awakening of religious thought, some rebellion in Jamestown, and even a representative government in Virginia. Witch-hunts, self-rule, and a constitution in Connecticut foreshadowed the future founding of the United States. However, after the French and Indian War, the honeymoon of salutary neglect came to an end.

HERE IS WHAT YOU NEED TO KNOW:
Definition: Indentured Servant

These were "adventurers" who traveled to the New World and settled mainly in Maryland and Virginia to work the tobacco fields. They generally labored for 7 years in exchange for the voyage over. They were given freedom dues (tools, land, etc) after their time was served.

Question: Near what waterway was much of Virginia's tobacco harvested?

Answer: Chesapeake Bay. Specifically, Jamestown was founded by a joint-stock company called *The Virginia Company* in 1607. They awarded *headrights*, or land grants, to spark immigration. If you see 1607 as a time frame on an essay, you are expected to write about Jamestown and the Chesapeake.

The bulk of tobacco farming took place near the Chesapeake Bay in the Maryland and Virginia area. Much of the work was done at first by indentured servants. Slaves would take over Southern fields soon after. It is important to know that indentured servants were farming tobacco *before* slaves.

Note: Southern colonies were settled for economic reasons. The Northern ones were predominantly religious settlements. Many died in the early years of settlement, as famine, disease, and conflict with Native

Definition: Bacon's Rebellion, 1676 (100 years before 1776)

Nathaniel Bacon led farmers in a rebellion against rich planters, the governor (William Berkeley), and Native Americans in Jamestown. The rebellion led to the burning of Jamestown, but fizzled out when Bacon died. It is significant because it is a colonial indicator of class struggle and political discontent in the United States, 100 years before its founding.

Question: Puritans or Pilgrims...who were the separatists?

Answer: Puritans were ***non-separatists***. They did not separate from the King of England who was the head of the Church. They settled at Massachusetts Bay under **John Winthrop** to establish a religious community known as a "city upon a hill."

Pilgrims were ***separatists***. They settled in Plymouth, Massachusetts and separated from the Church of England.

Tip: On Thanksgiving, people like to <u>separate</u> their turkey from their stuffing as they talk about the story of the Pilgrims. Pilgrims also liked to separate.

Definition: Halfway Covenant

Because there was diminished religious participation in colonial America, Puritans eased up on the qualifications for church membership. As long as one parent was a baptized and converted churchgoing participant, a person could join a church.

Definition: Anne Hutchinson and antinomianism

Anne Hutchinson questioned the Puritan religious establishment of Massachusetts Bay. She believed that faith alone was critical for salvation. This is known as antinomianism. She was banished for challenging church authority in 1637.

Definition: Salem Witch Trials, 1692

In 1692, young Puritan girls were accused of witchcraft, which was illegal in Massachusetts Bay. After fingers pointed in every direction, nineteen of the accused were executed. The significance of the trials is more important, as this was an early case of mass hysteria. In an essay about the Red Scare of 1919, or McCarthyism of the 1950s, a reference to witch-hunts in colonial times could go a long way.

Definition: Metacom/King Philip's War

There was a war fought from 1675-1676 (same year as Bacon's Rebellion) between the colonists and Native American tribes of New England who were united by Metacom (King Philip). The colonists ultimately defeated Metacom, but the conflict destroyed many Puritan towns and the economies within. A different conflict you should know about is the *Pequot War*, where colonists teamed up with Native Americans to defeat and deplete New England's Pequot Indian population.

Question: What colony was founded for religious freedom?

Answer: Rhode Island

Roger Williams founded Rhode Island as a religious retreat for persecuted people such as Jews and Quakers. Its early neighbors castigated the colony as "Rogue" Island. The oldest synagogue in the US still stands in Newport.

Question: What religious sect did William Penn found Pennsylvania for?

Answer: Quakers

Pennsylvania had no established church. Also important to know is Maryland's *Act of Toleration*, which granted freedoms to Christian sects.

Definition: Great Awakening

Even after the halfway covenant, religion was losing its influence in New England. The Great Awakening was a religious revival in the mid-1700s. Led by *George Whitefield* and *Jonathan Edwards*, the movement expressed theatrical emotion towards religion, and condemned sinners. New Lights, or those who favored the movement, looked to eliminate sin from the colonies through the lessons of the scriptures of both the Old and New Testament. Presbyterians and Baptists increased in number. Quakers were unaffected.

Still, many colonists were *Deists* who believed that God created the world, and then allowed natural law to take over.

Definition: John Peter Zenger Trial, 1735

The court's decision from this trial affirmed freedom of the press in the New York colony. Journalist John Peter Zenger was put on trial for printing something negative about colonial governor William Cosby. Zenger's attorney, Andrew Hamilton (not Alexander) argued that if something printed was true, then it can't be libel (libel means *false* printed statements). The jury agreed. Zenger was not guilty.

Definition: Middle Passage

The Middle Passage was the *Triangular Trade's* journey which brought slaves from Africa to the Caribbean. As for the Triangular Trade, molasses from the Caribbean was brought to New England, distilled into rum, and then traded to African kings for the slaves. The Trans-Atlantic Slave Trade would not be phased out until 1808.

Definition: Stono Rebellion, 1739

In South Carolina, there were rumors of slaves escaping to Spanish-controlled Florida to receive freedom. A slave named Jemmy recruited others in South Carolina looking for "liberty." They gained ammunition from a local shop, and went on a killing spree. Whites in the area returned fire, and the rebellion ended. It led to slave codes, such as the Negro Act of 1740, which prevented slave assembly, education, and property ownership.

Question: What should I know about Spanish settlements?

Answer: Spanish conquistadors were the first to arrive in the New World. *They brought domesticated horses.* By the colonial era, they were still on the continent. Whereas the French tended to ally with Native Americans for fur trading, the Spanish conquered them and had offspring. Spanish settlements were strong in:

1. Florida - St. Augustine was settled in 1565, and today is the oldest city in North America.

2. New Mexico - Santa Fe became a capital. Pueblo Indians revolted against Spanish rule and the spread of Christianity. Many Spaniards resettled in Texas.

3. California - The Spanish continued to spread Christianity throughout the western portion of North America. The Franciscan Order set up 21 outposts/religious centers known as *missions*.

Question: What colony had the first constitution?

Answer: Connecticut in 1639. The *Fundamental Orders of Connecticut* were written as the first constitution of its kind in the colonies.

Definition: House of Burgesses, 1619

England's Virginia Company allowed Virginians to elect representatives to a legislature. The House of Burgesses became the first representative government in the New World, and a model for the future Legislative Branch of the United States.

Definition: Mayflower Compact, 1620

The Pilgrims pledged justice, equality, majority rule, and direct democracy on the voyage over on the Mayflower. This is yet another example of self-government in the New World. In some places in New England, *town meetings* of local propertied men created laws.

Definition: Mercantilism

Mercantilism is an economic system where the European Mother Country (in this case, England), extracted the raw materials produced by its colonies and sold them finished goods. The sole purpose of the colonies was to make the Mother Country rich and self-sufficient.

Before the American Revolution, a series of *Navigation Acts* stated that the colonies had to exclusively trade certain items, like sugar and tobacco, with Britain. All trade had to be done on British or colonial ships, and goods destined for other nations had to first go through British hands. The Navigation Acts weren't enforced extensively until 1764, and smuggling was common.

Definition: Salutary Neglect

Because the British were thriving from mercantilism, they were willing to look the other way when it came to certain trade laws, and the governing affairs of the colonies (the expression was "let sleeping dogs lie"). This process, known as salutary neglect, ended after the French and Indian War when the British needed more revenue.

Question: What major events do I need to know about the French and Indian War, 1754-1763?

Answer: Remember, the colonists *are* British in this war! The British are the good guys! The British and colonists were fighting the French and Native Americans who had united to create a profitable fur trade. In Europe, the conflict was called the Seven Years War. *Note:* Not all Native Americans supported the French, as the Iroquois Confederacy—made up of the Six Nations of the Mohawks, Oneidas, Onondagas, Cayugas, Senecas, and Tuscaroras—sided with the British.

1. *The Albany Plan of Union*, 1754 - Benjamin Franklin had a belief that the colonies had to unite to win the French and Indian War. He created the famous "Join or Die" cartoon for this purpose. The plan failed in Albany, but the message stuck for centuries.

2. A young George Washington was engaged in conflict in western Pennsylvania at Fort Duquesne, near modern day Pittsburgh. He surrendered at Fort Necessity.

3. Battle of Quebec - William Pitt of Britain changed the war effort to concentrate more on Canada. The French lost at Quebec. Many of them now speak English.

4. Outcome of the War - The British formally controlled the 13 colonies and areas to the west. But, how were the British going to pay for such an expensive war? The following decades of taxation would help lead to the Revolutionary War. Salutary neglect was over.

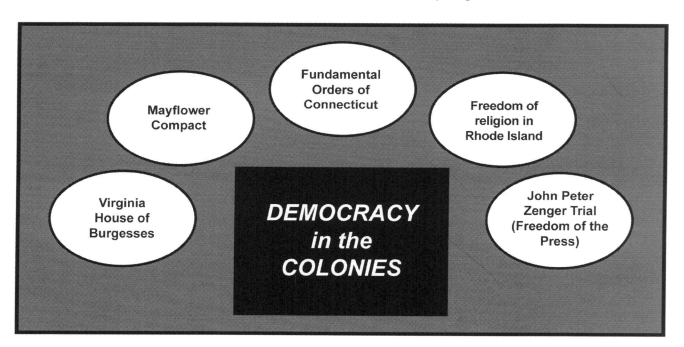

For a quick guide to Colonial Geography, see pg. 175

Review Questions

1. Anne Hutchinson created controversy in seventeenth century Massachusetts Bay society as she
   A) refused to baptize her eldest son
   B) renounced the Bible
   C) demanded rights for women
   D) attacked the authority of religious officials
   E) demanded the right to vote in village elections

2. The first years of the Jamestown settlement
   A) were successful in creating networks of trade for French fur
   B) proved to be dangerous and led to a large number of deaths
   C) created a bustling cotton economy supported by slave labor
   D) saw extensive political conflict
   E) increased Quaker populations in New England

3. Bacon's Rebellion displayed conflict between
   A) slave owners and slaves
   B) indentured servants and the British East India Company
   C) Native American tribes within Virginia and Maryland
   D) frontier tobacco farmers and the colonial governor
   E) tax collectors and American citizens

4. Deism is best explained as
   A) a decree that all events are destined to happen, and human action can not alter fate
   B) the belief that God had created the world, and then let natural law take over
   C) a disdain for materialism and a desire to find inner-peace
   D) a religious revival that was confined to Puritans living in Massachusetts Bay before 1700
   E) pagan beliefs in multiple gods

5. The primary labor force of Chesapeake Bay in the early seventeenth century was
   A) slaves
   B) indentured servants
   C) migrant laborers
   D) Native Americans
   E) Spanish adventurers

6. Rhode Island was settled by Roger Williams for
   A) fur trading and other commercial interests
   B) freedom of religion
   C) those who promoted a utopian community
   D) advocates for a bicameral legislature
   E) Puritans looking to settle on a "city upon a hill"

7. Compared to Puritans, the Pilgrims were
   A) loyal to the King of England
   B) the early preachers of the Great Awakening
   C) separatists
   D) only temporarily planning to stay in America
   E) always peaceful with Native Americans

8. Britain's policy of exploiting the colonies for their raw materials was known as

A) militarism

B) imperialism

C) mercantilism

D) antinomianism

E) industrialism

9. Which of the following was a result of the French and Indian War?

A) The Spanish increased their settlements in the northeast

B) A removal of Britain from the western lands of the Ohio River Valley

C) Decreased French presence in the colonies and Canada

D) English control of all land between the Atlantic and Pacific Oceans

E) Colonial independence from the Royal Crown

10. England did not interfere with colonial creations like the House of Burgesses or Great Awakening because

A) they supported freedom of religion

B) the distance between the two places prevented reliable communication

C) Britain believed in *no taxation without representation*

D) the colonies were profitable, and therefore social and political events were often overlooked

E) colonists who supported the British in the French and Indian War were rewarded with self-rule

Answers and Explanations

1. **D**. Anne Hutchinson disagreed with the way ministers were carrying out Puritan duties in Massachusetts Bay.

2. **B**. Many people died in the early years of the Jamestown settlement due to a lack of provisions and famine.

3. **D**. Nathaniel Bacon led a group of farmers who were angry at Governor William Berkeley for their low income and his favorable treatment of Native Americans.

4. **B**. Deists were numerous. Benjamin Franklin was considered by many to be one. They believed that God had created the universe, and then let natural law take care of it.

5. **B**. Indentured Servants were the first to come over as adventurers looking for economic gain near Chesapeake Bay. Slaves would be more abundant years later.

6. **B**. Rhode Island was settled as a religious sanctuary for people like Catholics or Jews. Some referred to it as "Rogue" Island.

7. **C**. Pilgrims were "separatists," meaning they separated from the King of England. Puritans were non-separatists who acknowledged the Crown as the head of the Church.

8. **C**. Mercantilism was the economic system whereby a Mother Country looked to extract all it could from its colonies.

9. **C**. France lost most of its land in the New World. After the Battle of Quebec, Britain gained a stronghold in Canada.

10. **D**. Salutary neglect refers to England's loose control over the colonies. As long as the system of mercantilism made England financially happy, Parliamentary laws would not be fully enforced. This hands-off approach kept England from meddling in many political and social movements as well.

Revolution and Constitution, 1763-1791

To pay for the costly French and Indian War, the British had to tax their subjects in America. The Stamp Act, Sugar Act, Townshend Acts... surely the colonists would understand the need to pay for the British Army...right? Gradually, the colonies pulled away from Britain, used their *Common Sense*, and declared independence. After losing many of the early skirmishes of the Revolutionary War, the Battle of Saratoga proved to be the turning point the Americans needed. After France and other European nations aided the cause for independence, Britain surrendered, and the 13 colonies became 13 states. But how would they legislate? After a failed Articles of Confederation, a strong and everlasting Constitution was ratified in 1788.

HERE IS WHAT YOU NEED TO KNOW:
Definition: Proclamation of 1763

This British law stated that colonists could not settle west of the Appalachian Mountains. The Americans were furious, but the British were attempting to protect them from Native American raids led by chiefs such as *Pontiac*. For the colonists, this would be one of the many arguments they would have with King George III and Parliament.

Definition: Sugar Act, 1764

As mentioned in the Colonial Era, the *Navigation Acts* were rarely enforced until 1764. That year, in an effort to raise money, British taxes were placed on imports of sugar. The Sugar Act intensified the cries of "no taxation without representation" that would be heard before the Revolutionary War. This statement meant that the colonists had no way to control British policy because they lacked seats in Parliament. But even with a seat, they would have been outvoted.

Definition: Stamp Act, 1765

A royal stamp had to be placed on the parchment of printed materials and official legal documents. Of course, that stamp was taxed. The Stamp Act was a *direct* and *internal* tax. The direct tax was added to the purchase price (like a sales tax). An internal tax was on items within the colonies (external taxes came on imports). The Stamp Act was repealed after colonists protested and Benjamin Franklin lobbied Parliament. Although the act was repealed, Parliament passed the 1766 *Declaratory Act* that affirmed Parliament's *"full power and authority to make laws...to bind the colonies...in all cases whatsoever."*

Definition: Townshend Acts, 1767

After the Stamp Act was repealed, Parliament passed the Townshend Acts (named for British official Charles Townshend). They were external and indirect taxes (included in the price) placed on imports such as paper and tea. To avoid these duties, many colonists smuggled. To combat smuggling, English customs agents investigated homes with *writs of assistance*, or permits (not court orders) for search and seizure.

Definition: Boston Massacre, 1770

This massacre began as a protest against British rule and taxes. It escalated into a mob in the streets of Boston. Things got out of hand when people hurled snowballs and rocks at the British troops. The soldiers fired guns, killing Bostonians such as Crispus Attucks (a free black). John Adams successfully defended the British troops in court. The event displayed the escalating tension in the area.

Two years later in 1772, another massacre occurred, this time to the crew of the British customs ship, the *Gaspee*. After the ship crashed into the shore in Rhode Island, it was boarded by colonists. They wounded some of the crew, looted the ship, and burned it.

Definition: Tea Act and Tea Party, 1773

The Tea Act actually did not raise prices, but it gave the British East India Company a monopoly in America. British tea was now available at a discount price (coupled with the small tax on tea from the Townshend Acts). However, the Americans resented such an action in principle. In addition, the act also upset local merchants who were trying to sell their own tea, as well as colonial middle men. So, led by Samuel Adams of the protest-organization *The Sons of Liberty*, colonists dressed up like Native Americans and dumped 342 cases of British tea into Boston Harbor.

Definition: Intolerable Acts of 1774

The Intolerable (or Coercive) Acts punished the colonists for the Tea Party. The Acts:

1. Closed Boston Harbor.

2. Decreased the power of the Massachusetts legislature.

3. Made colonists pay for the tea destroyed.

4. Issued a new *quartering act* (troops could stay in private homes).

5. The Quebec Act was passed as well which increased the size of Quebec, and the prevalence of Roman Catholicism in the region. The mostly Protestant colonists opposed this.

Definition: Committees of Correspondence

In the early 1770s, Samuel Adams reported about British activity to Massachusetts towns. Virginia would follow suit to create a chain of communication throughout the colonies.

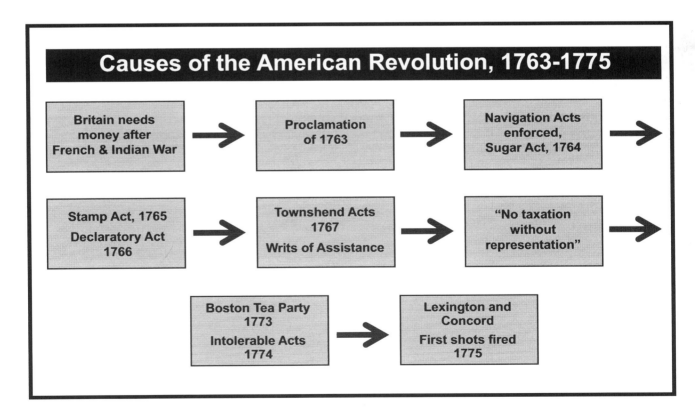

Causes of the American Revolution, 1763-1775

Britain needs money after French & Indian War → Proclamation of 1763 → Navigation Acts enforced, Sugar Act, 1764 →

Stamp Act, 1765 / Declaratory Act 1766 → Townshend Acts 1767 / Writs of Assistance → "No taxation without representation" →

Boston Tea Party 1773 / Intolerable Acts 1774 → Lexington and Concord / First shots fired 1775

Question: Where were the first shots of the Revolutionary War fired?

Answer: Lexington, and soon after, Concord, Massachusetts

These were two unorganized battles. Lexington was known as "the shot heard around the world." Although Paul Revere was captured in his ride warning of the attacking British, soldiers at Lexington were ready for battle. Still to this day, no one knows who fired first. Colonial *Minutemen* (who assembled within minutes) defended Lexington against the British Regulars. The war officially began, thus dividing colonists between American Patriots and British Loyalists or Tories.

Definition: Olive Branch Petition, July 1775

This was a last ditch effort to reconcile with King George III. The King was not receptive. To "extend the olive branch" means to ask for peace.

Definition: Continental Congress

There were two:

1. 1774, Philadelphia. Colonists protested both Parliament's actions and a lack of representation. Note: They were still loyal to the British Crown at this point.

2. 1775, Philadelphia. The colonists from New England wanted war. The Middle Colonies wanted more diplomacy. Still, the colonists prepared for war. George Washington was named Commander-in-Chief of the Continental Army.

Definition: Thomas Paine's *Common Sense*, 1776

Thomas Paine wrote an influential pamphlet where he said that it was *"common sense"* for America to be independent. After all, Britain is thousands of miles away, and is substantially smaller. *"Tis time to part."* His pamphlet was widely read, leading to increased demands for independence.

Definition: Egalitarianism

The spirit of the Revolution was egalitarianism...simply put, a fancy word for equality.

Question: What do I need to know about the Declaration of Independence of July 4, 1776?

Answer:

1. Enlightenment thought: "All men are created equal" with three unalienable rights..."life, liberty, and the pursuit of happiness." Remember, these are Enlightenment ideas stemming from *John Locke* in particular.

2. The document included a long list of grievances against King George III.

3. At the end, there was a formal declaration of war.

The document, written by Thomas Jefferson, declared independence, and that the United States was a free nation. Of course, it would mean nothing if the war with Britain was lost. All of the signers would have been tried for treason in that case, including John Hancock, whose signature was the largest.

Question: What Revolutionary War battles do I need to know?

Answer: The following tend to be the most important military events to know:

1. George Washington, commander of the Continental Army of *volunteers*, crossed the Delaware River in 1776 and won at Trenton, New Jersey, and later at Princeton, New Jersey.

2. Saratoga, New York in 1777 was the turning point. A few months after British General John Burgoyne surrendered to American Horatio Gates, the French signed an alliance with the United States. The French gave massive aid for the independence cause.

3. At Valley Forge, Pennsylvania in 1777-78, Washington held his army together in the winter, and recharged them for battle.

4. The final British defeat was at Yorktown, Virginia in 1781. General Charles Cornwallis surrendered his army to Washington.

Question: What famous foreigners helped the US out?

Answer:

1. Marquis de Lafayette - Young French aristocrat who came over and was like a son to Washington as his assistant.

2. Thaddeus Kosciuszko - Polish engineer who helped move artillery to the high ground at Saratoga.

3. Baron von Steuben - German officer known for his discipline and drilling of soldiers at Valley Forge.

Question: How on Earth did the United States win this thing?

Answer: Although England was a much stronger force…

1. The US had foreign help from France, Spain, and the Netherlands.

2. The US was fighting a defensive battle on their own soil.

3. Britain left much of its army in Europe because the continent was always in a flux of chaos.

4. The US had higher morale and a desire for independence. It is important to know that the American soldiers were volunteers. There would be no drafting of soldiers until the Civil War.

Definition: Treaty of Paris, 1783

This was the treaty that ended the war, and established the 13 colonies as 13 states. Benjamin Franklin was present to make sure the United States kept its land. John Adams was sent home from Paris because he didn't mingle well with the French diplomats. Thomas Jefferson replaced him and was better accepted.

Definition: Republican Motherhood

This was the idea that women should become educated, and teach their kids to honor civic duty and *republicanism*. The belief was that the republican virtues of the Revolution (liberty, equality, service) should be passed down to the next generation. As the keeper of the home, women were vital for the raising of good citizens.

Question: Who wrote the Articles of Confederation?

Answer: John Dickinson of Pennsylvania gets most of the credit. But Benjamin Franklin looked over the document.

The Articles were in effect from 1781-1789 (The Critical Period), and were the law of the land before the Constitution.

Question: What were some of the weaknesses of the Articles of Confederation?

Answer:

1. Each state could coin its own money.

2. No Executive Branch existed.

3. No regulation of interstate commerce.

4. No national court system.

5. No army.

6. 9 of the 13 states had to agree to pass a law.

7. All 13 states needed to agree to pass an amendment.

Definition: Shays' Rebellion, 1786-87

Daniel Shays' Rebellion was a Massachusetts uprising where farmers protested imprisonment for debt, lack of currency, and high taxes. It showed just how weak the Articles were, as there was no national army to put down the insurrection. The Massachusetts state militia eventually ended the violence, but plans to scrap the Articles intensified.

Definition: Land Ordinance of 1785 and Northwest Ordinance of 1787

These were two of the few accomplishments of the Articles. Both provided for future settlement in the west (today's Midwest). The Land Ordinance divided land into townships containing 36 sections for purchase. The Northwest Ordinance was of more importance, as it ***provided statehood*** for areas that reached 60,000 inhabitants. ***No slavery would be allowed in the Northwest Territories.***

Definition: Annapolis Convention

This was a meeting that decided to have another meeting. Only five states were represented here in Maryland. They determined that the Articles were weak, and further discussion would take place in Philadelphia in 1787.

Definition: Philadelphia Convention

Fifty-five delegates assembled in Philadelphia in 1787. ***Their intention was not to make a Constitution***, but rather to ***amend*** the Articles of Confederation. Of course, they would indeed write a new Constitution here.

Definition: Virginia Plan, New Jersey Plan, Great Compromise of the Convention

In a ***republic***, people are elected by the people, to serve the people. The Great Compromise created our modern day Legislative Branch that makes laws. It was based on:

The Virginia Plan - James Madison wanted a bicameral (2 house) legislature based upon population. The greater the population, the more representatives a state would have.

The New Jersey Plan - William Paterson wanted representation to be equal so the small states would not be under-represented.

The Great Compromise (Connecticut Compromise of Roger Sherman) – Created the current bicameral (2 house) legislature where the ***House of Representatives*** is based upon population, and the ***Senate*** has equal representation (2 Senators per state). A ***census*** taken every ten years determines state population and representation. Representatives were the only federal offices voted on by local citizens in the early years of the republic.

Definition: 3/5th Compromise

But wait a minute! If the House is based on population, how should the United States count slaves?

The Northern states wanted slaves to count for taxation, but not representation.

The Southern states wanted slaves to count for representation but not taxation.

Compromise - Each slave would count for 3/5th of a white person for both taxation and representation.

Note: The Trans-Atlantic Slave Trade could continue until 20 years after the Constitution (until 1808).

Definition: Commercial Compromise

The Northern states wanted a tax on imports and exports.

The Southern states wanted a tax on imports, but not exports, as they exported a lot of farm goods.

The compromise gave the federal government the power to tax imports but not exports. This tax on imports is referred to as a ***tariff***. Sometimes the term *customs duties* is used instead.

Definition: Federalists/Anti-Federalists

Federalists favored the Constitution and were led by James Madison, George Washington, and Alexander Hamilton.

Anti-Federalists were scared that the Constitution might put too much power in the hands of the government. They were led by James Winthrop, John Hancock, George Clinton, and George Mason.

Note: Jefferson (in France), and John Adams (in Great Britain) were not present for the debate.

Question: What was written to persuade New Yorkers and other doubters to ratify the Constitution?

Answer: *The Federalist* (or The Federalist Papers) was a series of 85 published essays that argued the need for a strong Constitution.

Alexander Hamilton wrote most of them. John Jay wrote a few on foreign policy. But, James Madison wrote the most famous one, Federalist #10 (see below).

Definition: Federalist #10

James Madison contended that the Constitution would work in a large republic. He believed that a strong union would be able to control tyrannical *factions*, or groups who were out for their own good. He believed that a republic that serves the public good could eliminate smaller factions, and the Constitution would further limit their effects.

Definition: Bill of Rights, 1791

Ultimately the Constitution was ratified (approved) in 1788 when 9 of the 13 states agreed. But the promise for a Bill of Rights was critical. It would become the first 10 Amendments (changes/additions) to the Constitution. The Bill of Rights protected important freedoms such as speech, right to bear arms, due process, prevention of cruel and unusual punishment, and the right to an attorney. The ones you need to know the most are in the No Bull Review Sheet, and will be addressed later in court case explanations.

Note: The Bill of Rights was ratified in 1791, two years after the Constitution went into effect.

Question: This is not a government class, but should I know anything about government?

Answer: Yes! If you know how government works, then you can skip this and move on.

Reflecting French philosopher Baron de Montesquieu's theory of *separation of powers*, the Legislative Branch (House and Senate) makes laws, the Executive Branch (President) enforces laws, and the Judicial Branch (Supreme Court) interprets them (makes sure they are fair). You need to know the following to understand some historical events in the curriculum:

1. *Federalism* is the division of power between the federal government and the states. The Congress has *delegated, or enumerated, powers* and can do big things like declare war and coin money. According to the Tenth Amendment, the states have *reserved powers*, and control education, marriage, and driving laws. For this course, know that the states controlled drinking laws, and women's ability to vote before their respective amendments. Some powers are shared, like taxation. These are called *concurrent powers*.

2. Nine-word phrase on how a bill becomes a law: *Passed by House, Passed by Senate, Signed by President*.

3. The *Electoral College*, rather than the American people directly, determines who becomes President. On Election Day, people vote for *electors* who have sworn to vote for a candidate. The number of Electoral Votes a state has is equal to the number of Representatives plus two, for the two Senators each state has. You need to know that to win a Presidential Election, a candidate must receive a majority of all possible Electoral Votes. Popular votes are irrelevant. If no candidate gets a majority

(which today is 270), then the House of Representatives chooses the President.

4. The Supreme Court is the highest court in the land. It can strike down acts of the other branches seen as unconstitutional. The power to do so is called *judicial review*. They can also overturn decisions from the highest state courts.

5. The House of Representatives can impeach a federal official. This means to charge with a crime. The Senate can then kick them out of office.

6. Congress also has a delegated power to do anything "necessary and proper." This allows the Constitution to grow over time, so it doesn't become a dated document. This power is found in the *Elastic Clause*. (described more in-depth later).

7. Each branch looks over the shoulders of the other two to make sure that there are no abuses of power. You need to know certain *checks and balances*. Here are a few major points.

If the President (Executive Branch) doesn't like a bill, it can be *vetoed* to prevent it from becoming a law. The Legislative Branch can then override that veto with a 2/3 vote. The President appoints federal offices like Supreme Court justices. The Senate then approves these appointments. The President can make treaties, but the Senate must approve them. The President is Commander-in-Chief of the military which can enforce laws. The chart below contains the most important checks and balances to know about.

Checks and Balances

	LEGISLATIVE	EXECUTIVE	JUDICIAL
LEGISLATIVE CHECKS		1. Can override vetoes by 2/3 vote 2. Senate can refuse to confirm a Presidential appointment	1. Can change the size of the Supreme Court
EXECUTIVE CHECKS	1. Can veto bills 2. Can call Congress into special session		1. Appoints Supreme Court justices 2. Grants pardons and reprieves
JUDICIAL CHECKS	1. Can declare an act of Congress to be unconstitutional (judicial review)	1. Can declare an act of the President to be unconstitutional	

Review Questions

1. Benjamin Franklin went to Britain to dispute which of the following?
   A) Stamp Act
   B) Proclamation of 1763
   C) Tea Act
   D) Sugar Act
   E) Quartering Act

2. The Proclamation of 1763
   A) created an indirect tax on all imports
   B) denied colonists the right to settle west of the Appalachian Mountains
   C) made all colonists open their homes to Writs of Assistance
   D) closed Boston Harbor
   E) taxed colonists without permitting their representation in Parliament

3. All were part of the Declaration of Independence EXCEPT:
   A) Grievances against King George III
   B) A formal declaration of war
   C) Enlightenment theory similar to John Locke
   D) A belief in a system of checks and balances
   E) A preamble

4. Republican motherhood affirmed that women should
   A) be given the right to govern in the colonies
   B) vote in Presidential Elections
   C) become educated and raise their children to be contributing members of society
   D) aid the Continental Army by knitting flags and uniforms, and providing food to those in need
   E) decrease the amount of alcohol consumption in the home

5. Why was the battle of Saratoga the turning point of the Revolutionary War?
   A) The victory led to an alliance with France
   B) Charles Cornwallis lost the largest part of his army
   C) George Washington finally controlled Canada
   D) The Ohio River Valley was now open for Spanish aid
   E) The British finally departed New York

6. The Northwest Ordinance of 1787 looked to
   A) remove British soldiers from the west
   B) establish new farming opportunities for settlers
   C) expand slavery into the west
   D) assume all state debts
   E) provide a plan for the incorporation of new states

7. Shays' Rebellion revealed what flaw of the Articles of Confederation?
   A) The presence of a strong Executive Branch
   B) There were no interstate courts
   C) The capital of the US was too far South
   D) There was no regulation of interstate commerce
   E) Absence of a national army

8. All of the following were a part of the Constitution ratified in 1788 EXCEPT:
   A) A bicameral legislature
   B) The Bill of Rights
   C) Elastic Clause
   D) Ability to declare war
   E) Power to tax imports

9. The 3/5th Compromise looked to
  A) determine the value of a slave on the national census
  B) eliminate slaves as a means to calculate representation
  C) decrease the number of Native Americans involved in representation
  D) allow a certain amount of African Americans to legislate in state constitutional conventions
  E) set up a taxation plan for imports of finished goods

10. The Constitution as it was ratified in 1788 provided for which of the following?
  A) Direct election of Senators
  B) Abolition of slavery north of Missouri
  C) Representatives of the House of Representatives to be chosen in local elections
  D) Presidents to be chosen directly by the people
  E) A formal Bill of Rights

Answers and Explanations

1. **A**. The Stamp Act was repealed after Benjamin Franklin went to England on behalf of colonists who dissented with the tax. The Townshend Acts soon replaced the Stamp Act.

2. **B**. The Proclamation was put in place to protect colonists from Native American raids from leaders such as Pontiac. The colonists were upset that they couldn't acquire more land.

3. **D**. Checks and Balances would be a part of the Constitution, not the Declaration of Independence.

4. **C**. The idea of republican motherhood meant that as care provider of the family, women would do their best to ensure the education of the future good citizens of the republic.

5. **A**. Benjamin Franklin made a 1778 alliance with France after General Burgoyne surrendered to American Horatio Gates at the battle of Saratoga.

6. **E**. According to this Ordinance, when territories received 60,000 inhabitants, they could apply for statehood.

7. **E**. Daniel Shays led a rebellion of discontented farmers in Massachusetts. It got out of control, thereby exposing the new government's lack of a military presence.

8. **B**. The Bill of Rights was added in 1791. The Constitution was ratified in 1788 with only the promise of a Bill of Rights.

9. **A**. For representation and taxation purposes, one slave counted as 3/5 of a white person when a census was taken. A census is a population count that is taken every ten years to determine representation.

10. **C**. Citizens could only vote for representatives in the House. Senators were not chosen by the people until 1913. The Electoral College still casts its vote for the President today.

The New Republic, 1789-c1823

(c, an abbreviation for the Latin circa, *will be used in this book to approximate time periods)*

The New Republic was a time period from roughly 1789-1823 (or George Washington's Inauguration to James Monroe's Doctrine). The country was fragile. Would the American experiment work? Washington's Presidency was full of walking on foreign policy eggshells. His financial advisor, Alexander Hamilton, presented a new financial plan that included a national bank. To Washington's chagrin, political parties began to emerge, leaving Federalists (Hamiltonians) battling Democratic-Republicans (Jeffersonians). After nearly going to war with France and limiting free speech of the American people, Federalist President John Adams lost the Election of 1800 to Democratic-Republican, Thomas Jefferson. However, Jefferson would legislate like a Federalist. So too at times would his Democratic-Republican successor, James Madison. After the War of 1812 ended in a stalemate, President James Monroe took over and looked to eliminate foreign influences from the Western Hemisphere.

HERE IS WHAT YOU NEED TO KNOW:
Question: What were some of the precedents of George Washington's Presidency?

Answer: A precedent means things borrowed by future Presidents.
1. A two term limit.
2. Neutrality in foreign affairs.
3. Formation of a cabinet to aid him in decisions.
4. A farewell address upon leaving office.

Question: Where were the three capitals of the United States?
Answer:
1. New York City 1789-1790

2. Then, it temporarily moved to Philadelphia (1790-1800), but…

3. After James Madison, Thomas Jefferson, and Alexander Hamilton had a fateful dinner, the capital was moved to Washington, DC. At the dinner, it was agreed that the capital would move south in exchange for state debts being assumed by the federal government. The paying off of Revolutionary War debts favored Northern states, as the South did not owe as much money. The Dinner Compromise, formally called the Compromise of 1790, was also important to the South because slavery could now exist in the nation's capital.

Question: Who was in Washington's first cabinet?

Answer: A cabinet is a collection of advisors.
1. Secretary of State (deals with foreign affairs) - Thomas Jefferson
2. Secretary of the Treasury (deals with financial affairs) - Alexander Hamilton
3. Secretary of War (deals with the military) - Henry Knox

Question: What made up Hamilton's financial plan?

Answer: In short, Hamilton wanted to:
1. Pay off all debts, foreign and domestic, by issuing new bonds to cover old debts. He believed that owing an immense debt would weaken the nation's economic reputation.
2. Support a national bank to monitor and control the money supply. It favored the wealthy, as stockholders controlled the bank. It was passed by virtue of the *Elastic Clause*. The Elastic Clause allows Congress to do anything they see as "necessary and proper." This creates a *loose interpretation* of the Constitution, and gives government more power to legislate. *Strict con-*

struction/interpretation would be the opposite, and would limit the government's power. Note: Loose interpretation, or *implied powers*, can be used by all three branches of government. The Elastic Clause itself is a Congressional entity.

3. Support taxes on imports and luxury items such as whiskey.

Question: What were the differences between the Hamiltonians and Jeffersonians?

Answer: For most of it, remember that you made safe plans…**SAFE PLANS**

Jefferson = favored **S**tates' rights or **S**trict interpretation of the Constitution, **A**griculture, **F**rance over Great Britain, and the **E**ducated and common man…**SAFE**

Hamilton = favored the **P**ropertied and rich, **L**oose interpretation of the Constitution, an **A**rmy, **N**ational bank, and a **S**trong central government…**PLANS**

Differences Between Thomas Jefferson and Alexander Hamilton

Issue	Thomas Jefferson	Alexander Hamilton
Who should have power in government?	The educated/ commoners	The propertied aristocracy
Give most power to the:	States	Federal or Central Gov't. (Strong Federal Gov't.)
Constitutional Interpretation	Strict — Don't give the Federal Government too much power to legislate	Loose — Allow the Federal Government to do whatever is "necessary and proper"
Stance on Army	Against! Gives government too much power	For! Will make the government powerful
National Bank	Con: Favors the rich	Pro: Stabilizes the economy
Favored foreign nation	France — They supported our revolution	Great Britain — the strongest nation; similar heritage
Preferred Economy	Agriculture	Industry and Commerce

Definition: Whiskey Rebellion, 1794

In 1794 "moonshiners" in western Pennsylvania were defying Hamilton's whiskey tax. They began an armed protest. Washington, as Commander-in-Chief, sent in the army to end the rebellion. This is significant. Compared to Shays' Rebellion which exposed the absence of an army under the Articles of Confederation, this insurrection was peacefully put down by the stronger government that existed under the Constitution.

Definition: Neutrality

Neutrality means to stay out of foreign alliances and conflicts. This was Washington's foreign policy, as the new nation could hardly afford to fight a war. Going one step further would be *isolationism*. Isolation would mean cutting off all ties, including trade. However, Washington is associated with *neutrality*, which he stated in his 1793 ***Proclamation of Neutrality.***

Definition: John Jay's Treaty, 1794

John Jay's treaty with Great Britain was unpopular. First, it did not end *impressment*. Impressment was when Britain seized American sailors and forced them into the British navy (described more in-depth later). In addition, the treaty made the South pay a debt, and also made Britain the favored nation in terms of trade. This upset other countries, notably France. The treaty did promise to remove British troops from the west.

Definition: Citizen Genêt

Genêt was a French ambassador to the United States in the 1790s. He encouraged anti-British sentiment and the attacking of British ships. The government condemned Genêt, and his actions never amounted to much.

Definition: Thomas Pinckney's Treaty, 1795

Thomas Pinckney's treaty with Spain gave the United States navigation of the Mississippi River, and a right to trade in New Orleans.

Definition: Washington's Farewell Address

As he left office, Washington warned about forming alliances with foreign countries. He was also concerned about the rise of political factions at home.

Definition: Election of 1796

John Adams (Federalist) defeated Thomas Jefferson (Democrat-Republican). Jefferson became the Vice President because of a provision in the original Constitution that said the second place finisher would become VP. In a country that now had political parties, Adams' presidency was doomed from the start.

Definition: XYZ Affair, 1797

To smooth things out with the French after Jay's Treaty favored Britain, the United States sent Secretary of State John Marshall and others to France to protect peace. The only problem was, the French wouldn't let the Americans talk to a diplomat named Talleyrand unless a fee of $250,000 was paid. The Americans wouldn't pay, and this incident led to the ***Quasi-War***, or ***Undeclared War*** with France. Nothing ever became of it.

Definition: Alien and Sedition Acts, 1798

After the XYZ Affair, panic set in for Adams and the Federalists. The Alien and Sedition Acts were four separate laws that limited free speech against the government, and allowed the President to deport undesirables who were suspected of plotting against the United States. The acts were a black eye for the Adams Administration, and might have led to his losing re-election. Note: The President can suspend habeas corpus in a time of war and arrest without due process.

Definition: Virginia and Kentucky Resolutions, 1798-99

Arguing for states' rights and strict interpretation of the constitution, Vice President Thomas Jefferson (Kentucky Resolution) and James Madison (Virginia Resolution) secretly wrote these statements in response to the Alien and Sedition Acts. They wrote that state legislatures *should* have the right to declare acts of the federal government "null and void." That idea, of course, would go against the very fabric of the Constitution itself. Unlike similar ideas penned later, these were created as protests against the Federalist Party, rather than an argument for disunion. Here is the time-line of events:

Definition: Election of 1800

The Election of 1800 was a mess. Jefferson had more Electoral Votes than Adams, but he was tied with Aaron Burr. Burr was supposed to be Jefferson's Vice Presidential candidate. But Burr did not step aside, and the election went to the House of Representatives. With recommendations from his old foe Hamilton, Jefferson was chosen President. In 1804, Burr assassinated Hamilton in a duel for unrelated reasons. Burr would later be involved in a failed plot to get part of the country to secede (leave the Union).

Definition: Twelfth Amendment

Because of the chaos stemming from the Election of 1800, this amendment stipulated that the President and Vice President shall run together on the same ticket. This way, it's evident as to which candidate is running for what office.

Definition: Revolution of 1800

The Revolution of 1800 was the nickname for Jefferson's Presidential victory. The Democratic-Republicans, the party thought to represent the average citizen, peacefully took power from the Federalists.

Definition: Louisiana Purchase, 1803

Looking to gain control of New Orleans for agricultural trade, President Jefferson found a better deal. He used implied powers (loose interpretation of the Constitution) to purchase the enormous territory of Louisiana from France's Napoleon Bonaparte. The US paid $15 million in a purchase made *via a treaty ratified by the Senate*. Although the deal would double the size of the country, Jefferson was forced to act like a Federalist to secure it. Note: He did *not* use the Elastic Clause! Congress utilizes that, *not* the President. Loose interpretation can be used without the Elastic Clause.

Definition: Lewis and Clark

Meriwether Lewis and William Clark explored the new Louisiana Territory, and went as far as the Pacific Ocean on the Oregon Trail. They received help from a young Native American, Sacagawea. By the way, she did not speak English! Her husband could translate her language into French.

Question: Where was the first overseas battle for the United States?

Answer: Tripoli
Jefferson sent gunboats to Tripoli (Libya) to

defeat the Barbary Pirates that were disrupting American trade in the Mediterranean Sea.

Definition: John Marshall and *Marbury v. Madison*

Supreme Court Chief Justice John Marshall increased the power of the federal government. More importantly, he was known for *judicial review,* which is the Supreme Court's power to review a law and determine if it is constitutional or unconstitutional. In *Marbury v. Madison*, Marshall and the Court declared the Judiciary Act of 1789 unconstitutional. If you want more information:

John Adams appointed Federalist "midnight judges" in the last days of his Presidency which were created by the Judiciary Act of 1801. He wanted to make these appointments before the Democratic-Republicans took office. Federalist William Marbury never received his job commission from the next Secretary of State, James Madison. He went to the Supreme Court to get a *writ of mandamus* (court order to force Madison to deliver his appointment). Although the Judiciary Act of 1789 said one could obtain a writ, the Constitution said nothing about going directly to the Supreme Court for such a matter. Hence, the law was unconstitutional.

Note: Jefferson hated the Federalist Supreme Court, and attempted to get Federalist judges, like Samuel Chase, impeached and removed from office. He was not successful.

Definition: Embargo Act (1807)

OGRABME! (That's "Embargo" spelled backwards in a famous political cartoon). Jefferson wanted to keep the United States neutral by cutting off trade to Europe. Outlawing exports was an unpopular idea that hurt his Presidency. The Embargo Act would be repealed after widespread protest in the northern states.

Here's how it was gradually repealed:

1809 - The Non-Intercourse Act allowed the US to trade with countries other than Britain and France.

1810 - Macon's Bill Number 2 allowed the US to trade with Britain and France if they respected US neutrality.

Question: What were the causes of the War of 1812 with Britain?

Answer:

1. Impressment of sailors. The British were seizing Americans who were presumed deserters of the British navy, and forcing them into service for Britain. Note: Some were indeed deserters, others were not. The notable incident of impressment was the *Chesapeake-Leopard Affair* of 1807. The *Chesapeake* was boarded by the British, and four members of the crew were captured.

2. A quest for more land, particularly Canada.

3. A desire to finally remove Britain from the American northwest. (They never really left.)

Question: What should I know about the war itself?

Answer:

1. Washington, DC, including the White House (then called the Executive Mansion or Palace), was burned by the British.

2. Old Ironsides, the USS *Constitution*, fought legendary naval battles.

3. Andrew Jackson became a hero at the Battle of New Orleans, which ironically was fought in 1815 after...

4. The Treaty of Ghent was signed in 1814, which ended the war with no land changes.

5. War Hawks wanted war...Doves wanted peace.

6. President James Madison favored a conscription act (draft), but troops were not draft-

ed into this war.

Question: What were the results of the War of 1812?

Answer:

1. Increased nationalism (Francis Scott Key wrote his poem, *The Defence* (old English spelling) *of Fort McHenry*, that eventually became our National Anthem, while watching the bombardment).

2. Death of the Federalist Party after the Hartford Convention (which will be explained next).

3. Increased manufacturing.

4. Increased isolationism.

Development of US Political Parties

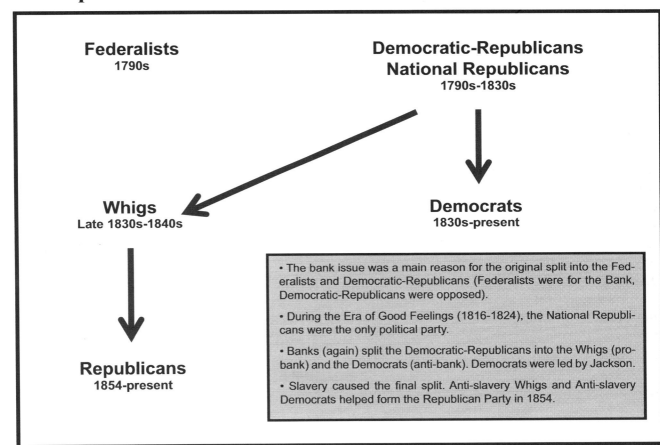

Federalists
1790s

**Democratic-Republicans
National Republicans**
1790s-1830s

Whigs
Late 1830s-1840s

Democrats
1830s-present

Republicans
1854-present

- The bank issue was a main reason for the original split into the Federalists and Democratic-Republicans (Federalists were for the Bank, Democratic-Republicans were opposed).

- During the Era of Good Feelings (1816-1824), the National Republicans were the only political party.

- Banks (again) split the Democratic-Republicans into the Whigs (pro-bank) and the Democrats (anti-bank). Democrats were led by Jackson.

- Slavery caused the final split. Anti-slavery Whigs and Anti-slavery Democrats helped form the Republican Party in 1854.

Definition: Hartford Convention, 1814-15

The Federalists assembled in New England to voice their displeasure with the War of 1812 (which was rather popular elsewhere). They talked about Northern secession, and then their party broke up. This was the end of the Party of Hamilton.

Definition: Era of Good Feelings

After the War of 1812 and the disappearance of the Federalist Party, the Republicans (Democratic-Republicans) were the only major political party until c1824. We will refer to the chart above throughout the book to explain political parties during the nineteenth century.

Definition: American System

Kentuckian Henry Clay had a belief that America could self-sufficiently sustain itself, as there was enough agriculture and industry to remain isolated from Europe. High tariffs would protect American jobs, a national bank would control finances, and an internal improvements bill would support infrastructure with new roads and bridges. The full idea never happened, as his internal improvements bill was not passed.

Definition: Adams-Onis Treaty, 1819

This was Secretary of State John Quincy Adams' treaty that led to the purchase of Florida. Be sure to note that Andrew Jackson, then in the military, also fought in the Seminole Wars in Florida to secure the land for the US.

Question: Besides *Marbury v. Madison*, what other Supreme Court decisions of John Marshall were important?

Answer: The following cases all led to a ***strengthening of the federal (national) government***.

1. *McCulloch v. Maryland*, 1819 - Because the State of Maryland wanted to get rid of a branch of the Bank of the United States, it put a tax on its banknotes. Marshall ruled that a state could not tax a federal entity. He said that the power to tax meant "the power to destroy."

2. *Gibbons v. Ogden*, 1824 - Thomas Gibbons was issued a license from the *federal government* for steamship commerce between New York and New Jersey. Aaron Ogden was issued a similar license from *New York State*. Marshall said that Gibbons had the legitimate license, because the federal government regulated interstate commerce (commerce between different states). Thus, Marshall upheld the supremacy of the federal government.

3. *Cohens v. Virginia,* 1821 - Marshall contended that the US Supreme Court could review higher court decisions of the states. Throughout American History, state decisions would be overturned by the Supreme Court. Again, Marshall was extending the federal government's power over the states.

4. *Fletcher v. Peck*, 1810 - State legislators in Georgia were bribed into selling a large chunk of land near the Yazoo River (Mississippi). When the next legislature in Georgia came to power, they wanted the land back. Marshall ruled that although the contract was scandalous, it had to be honored. Contracts were binding.

5. *Dartmouth College v. Woodward*, 1819 - New Hampshire wanted to change the charter of Dartmouth College which dated back to the days of King George III. Similar to the *Fletcher* case, Marshall stood by the original contract.

Definition: Monroe Doctrine

President Monroe aligned with Britain to prevent other European nations from colonizing, or meddling in the affairs of countries in the Western Hemisphere. In particular, this was created over concerns that some recent independent countries of Latin America might fall back into the hands of Spain.

Review Questions

1. George Washington's Farewell Address advocated for which of the following?
   A) Continued alliance with France
   B) Acknowledgement of Spain as the favored nation for trading
   C) A hope that the Federalists and Democratic-Republicans would cooperate to form the next cabinet
   D) Ending the Commercial Compromise
   E) Refraining from making permanent alliances with nations abroad

2. Alexander Hamilton supported all of the following EXCEPT:
   A) paying off debt
   B) excise (luxury) taxes
   C) a national bank
   D) a national army
   E) strict interpretation of the Constitution

3. Which event led to the XYZ Affair with France?
   A) The Quasi-War
   B) Jay Treaty
   C) Alien and Sedition Act
   D) Virginia and Kentucky Resolutions
   E) Louisiana Purchase

4. The Alien and Sedition Acts of 1798 were designed to
   A) deport or censor anyone deemed to be dangerous to America
   B) keep the United States neutral from Napoleon
   C) balance the number of free and slave states in the Union
   D) keep immigrants from entering the country
   E) embargo any nations that followed a policy of impressment

5. President Thomas Jefferson acted like a Federalist in all of the following instances EXCEPT:
   A) The Embargo Act
   B) Use of the National Bank
   C) Attack on Tripoli and expansion of the navy
   D) Virginia and Kentucky Resolutions
   E) The Louisiana Purchase

6. All of the following were true of the court case *Marbury v. Madison* EXCEPT:
   A) John Marshall expanded the power of the court
   B) The concept of judicial review was implemented
   C) The Judiciary Act of 1789 was deemed unconstitutional
   D) William Marbury was never delivered his commission from James Madison
   E) It would be the only time until 1900 that an act of Congress would be declared unconstitutional

7. Thomas Jefferson favored the purchase of Louisiana because
   A) he was following the principles of his Federalist supporters
   B) Mississippi River navigation would open up new networks of trade
   C) removal of Native Americans to the west was vital for increasing industry
   D) he favored the creation of factories in the west
   E) it would open up an all-water route to the Pacific Ocean

8. The Hartford Convention was responsible for the
   A) death of the Federalist Party
   B) repeal of the Alien and Sedition Acts
   C) end to the Embargo Act
   D) peace treaty to end the War of 1812
   E) a formal alliance between America and France

9. In what Supreme Court decision was the supremacy of the federal government upheld with regards to interstate commerce?
   A) *Cohens v. Virginia*
   B) *Fletcher v. Peck*
   C) *Gibbons v. Ogden*
   D) *Marbury v. Madison*
   E) *Worcester v. Georgia*

10. The intention of the Monroe Doctrine of 1823 was to
   A) bring about a Mexican Revolution
   B) keep Latin America isolated from the United States mainland
   C) remove British influence from Venezuela
   D) prevent European nations from meddling in the affairs of the Western Hemisphere
   E) cut all ties to Haiti after the slave revolt of Toissaint L'Ouverture

Answers and Explanations

1. **E**. With help from Hamilton's pen, Washington warned about entanglements with foreign alliances abroad, and political party factions at home.

2. **E**. Hamilton was an advocate for ***loose*** interpretation of the Constitution, and use of the elastic clause.

3. **B**. After Jay's Treaty with Britain, the US needed to smooth over some bad feelings with France. When they sent over envoys, they were charged a bribe to speak with a French diplomat named Talleyrand. The Americans declined to pay and left.

4. **A**. In the wake of the XYZ Affair and Quasi-War with France, the Adams Administration looked to deport and censor Americans seen as disloyal.

5. **D**. Traditionally, Jeffersonian thought meant a favoring of states' rights. The Virginia and Kentucky Resolutions said just that. Years later as President, however, Jefferson acted like a Federalist at times.

6. **E**. The Supreme Court used judicial review (determining if acts of the Legislative or Executive Branch were unconstitutional) multiple times before 1900.

7. **B**. The Louisiana Territory doubled the size of the nation. The original objective though, was to gain control of New Orleans and the Mississippi River.

8. **A**. During the War of 1812, the Hartford Convention was held by the Federalists. After talks of secession in the North, the Federalist Party disappeared.

9. **C**. In *Gibbons v. Ogden* the court ruled that since Gibbons received his rights to operate ferries from the US Government, he therefore had a more legitimate claim than Ogden, who received his rights from the State of New York.

10. **D**. With the help of Britain, Monroe was able to enforce his doctrine to keep European nations from colonizing in the Western Hemisphere.

Jacksonian Democracy c1824-c1840

After losing the Election of 1824, the common man, Andrew Jackson, came back with a vengeance to win in 1828. Jackson was a loose cannon, and a powerful President. He enforced a tariff, vetoed the Bank, and removed Native Americans to west of the Mississippi River. Although associated with *Jacksonian Democracy*, he was notorious for appointing his friends and campaign supporters to office. Socially, the Age of Jackson included the *Age of Reform (see pg. 37)* where movements such as the Second Great Awakening, transcendentalism, and temperance spread throughout the nation. At the same time, an economic transformation, or market revolution, was happening in the North and West. Transportation and communication were becoming more accessible.

HERE IS WHAT YOU NEED TO KNOW:
Definition: Sectionalism

Sectionalism is the belief that one's loyalty should rest with their section of the country, rather than the nation as a whole. Here are the sectional loyalties you need to know from 1830-1850:

North	South	West
Most populous	Population part slave	Least populous
Supports the Bank	Hates the Bank	Split on Bank Issue
Industrial	Agricultural	Developing
Pro-Tariff. The tariff promotes industrial growth.	Anti-Tariff. The tariff raises prices, and the South mainly exports.	Split on tariff. Economy has both industry and agriculture.
Anti-slavery feeling growing by 1850	Pro-slavery	Split on slavery issue
Leader: Daniel Webster	Leader: John C. Calhoun	Leader: Henry Clay

Definition: Corrupt Bargain

In the Election of 1824, Andrew Jackson of Tennessee led John Quincy Adams in both the electoral and popular vote. But, since William Crawford and Henry Clay also received Electoral Votes, no man received the majority necessary to win. So, the election went to the House of Representatives. In an alleged backroom agreement, Henry Clay offered the House's support to Adams, so long as Clay could become the next Secretary of State. This agreement was later nicknamed by opponents as "The Corrupt Bargain." Clay always denied it. Nonetheless, Adams was a one term President.

Jackson would come back to win the Election of 1828. He was the first President to be from the West.

Question: What are the four main things to know about Andrew Jackson's Presidency?

Answer: **B-I-T-S**

B - **B**ank Veto

I - **I**ndian Removal Act

T - **T**ariff Enforcement

S - **S**poils System (all four will be explaned)

Definition: Spoils System

"To the victor belongs the spoils!" Back in the nineteenth century, those who helped a president's campaign expected to receive a nice cushy job in government. Jackson was notorious for such appointments. This practice would end in 1883 after the passage of the Pendleton Act.

Definition: Caucus and Nominating Convention

Originally, there was a *caucus system* where just a few party bosses sat in "smoke-filled rooms" (as they smoked cigars) to choose the candidates who would run in the November Presidential Election. New *Nominating Conventions* expanded democracy, as now common people were allowed to help nominate a future President. The Anti-Masonic Party had the first one in 1832. During Jackson's time, property requirements to vote began to lift.

Definition: Jacksonian Democracy

This was the belief that government should represent and be controlled by the ***common man***. It was similar to Jefferson's belief in political equality. With few exceptions, Jacksonian Democrats controlled the White House until the Civil War.

Alexis de Tocqueville was a French political writer who visited and wrote about life in the US. In 1835, he authored *Democracy in America*, in which he observed the equality and liberty being experienced by American citizens in the age of Jacksonian Democracy. He also commented on the importance of Christianity in the lives of the American people.

Definition: Kitchen Cabinet

Jackson's "Kitchen Cabinet" was a term coined by his opponents. They used it to describe the way Jackson would seek the opinions of advisors who weren't necessarily in his true cabinet.

Question: What do I need to know about the economic transformation of the early nineteenth century?

Answer: There was a "market revolution" in the early to middle nineteenth century.

1. First there were roads, like the National Road, or Cumberland Road, which went from Maryland to Illinois. Another word for road is ***turnpike.***

2. The ***Erie Canal*** was completed in 1825, and it linked the Midwest to the East in upstate New York. This led to more trade.

3. Railroads emerged by 1830. They were slow, but faster than road travel. The North and South had equal amounts of railroad track mileage until about 1850. After that, the North far exceeded the South.

4. On the water, steamboats were prevalent by 1830, and were based on Robert Fulton's technology.

5. Eli Whitney invented the ***cotton gin*** in

1793. This led to a greater demand for slaves, as Southern "King Cotton" became more profitable. Whitney also invented the system of *interchangeable parts*. This meant that if a part of a firearm broke, you could just replace that part…instead of the entire weapon.

6. *Samuel Slater* was seen as the "Father of the American Factory System," as he brought English textile machinery to the United States. In New England, the factory system emerged in places like *Lowell, Massachusetts*. Here, the company provided lodging for workers. The labor force of unmarried women, or *"mill girls,"* eventually gave way to Irish immigrants during the 1840s. New England had abundant harbors for trading raw materials and finished goods.

Question: Why did Jackson veto the re-charter of the Bank of the United States in 1832?

Answer: In his 1832 veto message, Jackson said he vetoed the Second Bank of the United States (successor to Hamilton's National Bank) because:

1. Foreigners had too much stock in the bank.
2. The bank favored the rich, and not the common man.

He also did not trust Nicholas Biddle, the head of the bank. Jackson thought he was corrupt.

Question: What is the difference between hard and soft money?

Answer:

Hard Money = gold and silver coins, also known as *specie*.

Soft Money = paper. Paper money can create inflation faster than hard money.

Paper was favored by bankers and people who purchased a lot of land known as *speculators*. It was not typically favored by *the com-*

mon man. Note: 60 years later, poor farmers will want inflation on crop prices during the age of Populism in the 1890s.

Question: What was the outcome of the Bank Veto?

Answer:

1. Money was taken out of the bank and put into "pet" banks (state banks loyal to Jackson).
2. The money found its way out of banks, and into people's pockets. Too many paper notes in circulation created inflation.
3. To control the inflation, Jackson issued the *Specie Circular* order in 1836, which stated that all federal lands had to be purchased in hard money (gold and silver).
4. That order made banknotes lose their value.
5. The economy spiraled out of control and the Panic of 1837 set in under President Martin Van Buren.

The next few decades saw a fight to put the government's money into an *independent treasury*. This meant keeping it in a place that did not function like a powerful bank.

Definition: Whig Party

Supporters of the Bank felt alienated by Jackson's veto. They believed that he was acting like a King. In Britain, those who did not support the King called themselves Whigs. The Whig Party in America was a new conservative creation that was anti-Jackson. *(See pg. 27)*

Definition: Peggy Eaton Affair

Most of Jackson's cabinet resigned because they hated Peggy Eaton, the wife of Jackson's Secretary of War John Henry Eaton. Jackson took her under his wing. Years before, Eaton was accused of adultery, and Jackson felt this was unwarranted. The treatment reminded him of similar accusations against his late wife. John

C. Calhoun resigned as Vice President partly over this "Petticoat Affair." Martin Van Buren would succeed him after the Election of 1832.

Definition: Tariff of Abominations, 1828

Review: A tariff, or protective tariff, is a tax on imports that inflates foreign prices to protect American jobs. The South had little use for a tariff because they didn't have many industrial jobs, and would have to pay higher prices on all finished goods (tariffs were known to raise domestic prices as well).

The 1828 tariff reached a very high level, leading to its southern nickname, "The Tariff of Abominations."

Definition: *South Carolina Exposition and Protest*, 1828

After the Tariff of Abominations, Vice President John C. Calhoun wrote the *South Carolina Exposition and Protest*. It stated that South Carolina and the Southern states *should* be able to nullify acts of Congress. This was written in the spirit of Jefferson and Madison's *Virginia and Kentucky Resolutions*. Calhoun, however, hinted at secession over the tariff, even at this early date.

Related to the subject, in 1830, Daniel Webster of Massachusetts debated Robert Hayne of South Carolina, attacking the idea of secession and disobeying federal law. Webster championed a firm union. This was the famous *Webster-Hayne Debate*.

Definition: Ordinance of Nullification, 1832

The Tariff of 1828 was replaced by the Tariff of 1832, whose rates the South still found too high. South Carolina held a special convention in which they passed the Ordinance of Nullification. This declared the tariffs of 1828 and 1832 "null and void."

Question: How was conflict avoided after the Ordinance of Nullification?

Answer: As the chief executor of federal laws, President Jackson threatened a *Force Bill* to shove the tariff down the throats of the South. However, before violence would ever occur, Henry Clay brokered a Compromise Tariff in 1833 that promised to gradually reduce tariffs over the next several years. Here is the sequence of events you need to know:

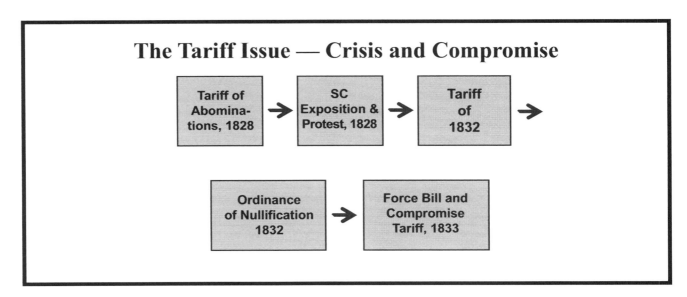

The Tariff Issue — Crisis and Compromise

Tariff of Abominations, 1828 → SC Exposition & Protest, 1828 → Tariff of 1832 →

Ordinance of Nullification 1832 → Force Bill and Compromise Tariff, 1833

Definition: Indian Removal Act of 1830

This was legislation that removed Native Americans from the east, and relocated them west of the Mississippi River (see Trail of Tears below).

Question: How did Jackson clash with the Supreme Court over Native American rights?

Answer: Here are the two cases you need to know:

Cherokee Nation v. Georgia (1831) - The Supreme Court ruled that because the Cherokee Indians of Georgia were not a foreign nation, they could not get original jurisdiction (have their case heard directly) at the Supreme Court. But...

Worcester v. Georgia (1832) - The Supreme Court ruled that Georgia could not pass legislation regarding Cherokee lands. Jackson defiantly said of Chief Justice John Marshall, "John Marshall has made his decision, now let him enforce it." Thus, there was a confrontation between the Executive and Judicial branches. But as a strong executive, Jackson held an edge over Marshall.

Definition: Trail of Tears

In the winter of 1837-38, approximately 15,000 Cherokee Indians were uprooted from Georgia. On the western voyage, thousands died from starvation and cold temperatures. Note: Jackson was out of office by then, as Martin Van Buren had become the new Commander-in-Chief. Still, it was Jackson's removal policy that associated him with this tragedy.

The Age of Reform: Social History c1830-c1850

Definition: Transcendentalism

This was mysticism and philosophy that helped a person find their true inner-self. The movement renounced materialism, embraced nature, and favored artistic achievement. Key writers were Ralph Waldo Emerson, Henry David Thoreau, and Walt Whitman. Thoreau, who was famous for his introspective writings of isolation at Walden Pond, believed in civil disobedience, or disobeying laws he saw as unjust.

Definition: Second Great Awakening

Yes, another Great Awakening. For this one you need to know:

1. It started in the "***burned over district***" in western New York near Rochester, with a man by the name of ***Charles Grandison Finney***. The movement was strong from about 1800-1850.

2. It was another religious revival that strongly encouraged faith.

3. There was a belief in a ***millennium*** (thousand years of peace where Jesus Christ would return to rule over the people).

4. There was a hope for ***perfectionism***, or faith in the human capacity to eliminate sin, and achieve a better life on Earth through conscious acts of will.

5. It increased the numbers of both Methodists and Baptists.

Movements affected by the Second Great Awakening included abolition, temperance, women's rights, public education, and utopian communities.

Definition: Temperance

Temperance was a movement in the mid-nineteenth century that looked to get rid of the consumption of alcohol. The issue gave an opportunity for women to enter the political world. Years later, the sale of alcohol would be prohibited (Eighteenth Amendment, 1919).

Definition: Seneca Falls Convention, 1848

This was a major women's convention that took place in upstate New York. Elizabeth Cady Stanton and Lucretia Mott were key leaders. They adopted a ***Declaration of Sentiments***, and concluded that "all men and women are created equal."

They challenged the ***cult of domesticity***, which stated that women were meant to be passive, virtuous, stay in the home, and be subservient to men. Women hoped to leave their ***sphere*** of the home, and have more political and economic opportunity.

Another woman important to know is ***Dorothea Dix***. She fought for the better treatment of mentally ill patients in asylums.

Definition: Horace Mann

Mann was a Massachusetts legislator who favored universal public education as a means to create a population of disciplined, good, young citizens. His plans began in Massachusetts and spread to other states. Under the laws of federalism (division of powers between the state and federal government), education is a reserved, or state power. So, public education was done on a state to state basis. Just try to remember, "Mann, did he love public education!"

Adults also received education, as traveling lecturers, speaking at ***lyceums*** (educational meetings), talked about everything from science to philosophy. The movement was founded by Josiah Holbrook. Ralph Waldo Emerson was known to speak at lyceum lectures.

Definition: Hudson River School

The Hudson River School was an art movement dedicated to the painting of nature *landscapes* near the Hudson River of upstate New York. The paintings, which exhibited *romanticism*, also reflected the exploration and settlement of nineteenth century America.

Definition: Shakers

The Shakers created a deeply religious movement that had elements of socialism. They lived isolated in a community of shared property with separation of the sexes (and no sexual relations). They renounced all aspects of sin.

Definition: Brook Farm/New Harmony

Brook Farm looked to become a *utopian community*. But a utopia was more of a hope than a reality. It aimed to have a perfect, self-sustainable, and isolated society. Brook Farm was founded by transcendentalist and Unitarian minister, *George Ripley*. People worked together for a common good and the survival of the community. Brook Farm had financial problems, and lasted less than a decade.

Robert Owen led the utopian community at New Harmony (Indiana). Founded in 1825, it was an attempt to find social perfection. This experiment was also short-lived.

Definition: Unitarians

Unitarians were Christians who believed that God existed only within Himself, and not in the Trinity. They believed that a doctrine of good deeds and works could lead to salvation.

Definition: Mormons

The Church of Jesus Christ of Latter-Day Saints was founded by *Joseph Smith*, who published the Book of Mormon in 1830. After Smith was murdered, *Brigham Young* led the Mormons to Utah where they established a religious community. The movement had thousands of followers who settled in the Utah Territory. Because the religion condoned polygamy (multiple wives), controversy stalled Utah from becoming a state.

Review Questions

1. All of the following were examples of Jacksonian Democracy in the first half of the nineteenth century EXCEPT:
   A) A belief in the common man
   B) Encouragement to take part in politics
   C) Nominating Conventions
   D) Decreasing aristocratic privileges
   E) Caucus systems

2. The famous debate between Daniel Webster and Robert Hayne centered around the issues of
   A) slavery and sectionalism
   B) state power and national union
   C) impressment and war with Britain
   D) shipping rights and the Embargo Act
   E) the national bank veto and transferring of funds into "pet" banks

3. Which of the following best illustrates Andrew Jackson's use of the spoils system?
   A) Support of the Second Great Awakening
   B) Vetoing of the Bank of the United States
   C) Appointing political supporters to office
   D) Belief in nominating conventions
   E) Enforcement of the Tariff of Abominations

4. In the *South Carolina Exposition and Protest*, John C. Calhoun emphasized the
   A) belief that states should be able to nullify laws of the federal government
   B) importance of the Bank of the United States in regulating the nation's money supply
   C) need for the Trans-Atlantic Slave Trade to continue after 1808
   D) understanding that Native Americans had to be removed west of the Mississippi River
   E) desire of Southern states to acquire cheap land in the west

5. The formation of the Whig party was in response to
   A) the Trail of Tears
   B) Andrew Jackson's veto of the Bank of the United States
   C) dissatisfaction regarding the Force Bill's infringement on Southern Rights
   D) The Tariff of Abominations
   E) The Peggy Eaton Affair

6. Dorothea Dix was best known for her work regarding
   A) those with mental illness
   B) birth control for women
   C) suffrage
   D) temperance
   E) abolition

7. The Erie Canal was instrumental in developing trade in the middle of the nineteenth century because
   A) the Ohio River Valley now had an outlet to the Mississippi
   B) Midwestern states could be financially linked to the east
   C) New York City and New Jersey could trade easier without navigating the Hudson River
   D) the Mississippi and Missouri rivers would be able to interconnect all parts of the nation
   E) it was the first of many successful applications of Henry Clay's American System

8. The Hudson River School created what type of art?
   A) Landscape paintings
   B) Abstract art
   C) Impressionism
   D) Sculpture
   E) Photography

9. Ralph Waldo Emerson and Henry David Thoreau would agree most in
    A) defending slavery
    B) individual reflection
    C) universal secondary education
    D) Native American removal
    E) high tariffs

10. The Second Great Awakening had an influence on all of the following movements EXCEPT:
    A) Education reform
    B) Abolition
    C) Temperance
    D) Safer working conditions
    E) Women's rights

Answers and Explanations

1. **E**. Jacksonian Democracy was supposed to bring more opportunity to the "common man." A caucus system did not give people a choice when selecting Presidential candidates.

2. **B**. Webster eloquently contested Hayne's belief that states did not have to listen to federal laws. The actual debate was about methods for securing land.

3. **C**. The spoils system meant appointing one's friends or campaign supporters to government offices.

4. **A**. Calhoun believed that states should be able to nullify federal acts like the tariff. South Carolina would do just that with the Ordinance of Nullification in 1832.

5. **B**. The first two splits in American political parties took place over the bank.

6. **A**. Dorothea Dix aided those with mental illness in asylums in the 1840s.

7. **B**. The Erie Canal was built in upstate New York to link trade between the East and the Midwest.

8. **A**. The Hudson River School involved people painting beautiful landscapes of the Hudson River in upstate New York.

9. **B**. Both men were transcendentalists who believed in introspective evaluation of one's character.

10. **D**. The Second Great Awakening led to social reform. Better working conditions and unionization were economic issues that weren't addressed until the second half of the nineteenth century.

Antebellum/Pre-Civil War, 1820-1860

Economic tension, slavery, political strife, ideological conflict, and ultimately the Election of Abraham Lincoln. All of these events led to Southern secession from the Union in 1860. Throughout the antebellum (pre-Civil War) era, Northerners and Southerners attempted to compromise their differences. However, because of manifest destiny and sectionalism, the Civil War proved inevitable. Throughout this time period, there was a growing movement to end slavery. From literature to violent actions, the abolition movement spread from the North to the West.

HERE IS WHAT YOU NEED TO KNOW:
Definition: Antebellum

Antebellum means the time-period before the Civil War. Again, don't forget the importance of *sectionalism* where loyalty rests with one's own section of the country rather than the nation as a whole. When you think "antebellum period," visualize 1820-1860.

Definition: Compromise of 1820/Missouri Compromise

This was Major Slave Legislation #1 of 3. The goal in the antebellum period was to keep a balance between slave and free states. So, when certain territories were ready for statehood, decisions had to be made. In this compromise:

1. Maine would enter as a free state.
2. Missouri would enter as a slave state, but...
3. After the admission of Missouri, no slavery would be allowed north of the 36° 30' latitude line within the Louisiana Territory.

Henry Clay of Kentucky, "The Great Compromiser," received credit for this legislation.

Question: In short, what do I need to know about slave life?

Answer: The economy of the South was based on slaves working on plantations. Regarding slavery:

1. Paternalism was the relationship between slave and master. It was similar to that of child to parent.
2. Only a very small percentage of people owned slaves before the Civil War. Surprised? Statistics on this vary but about, 6-7% of people, or 25% of families had slaves in the South. Even smaller were statistics of those who owned multiple slaves. Most of the Southern population was comprised of poor *yeoman* farmers. The lack of slave-owners is a very important fact to know.
3. Slaves held onto their African culture in music, but combined it with Christianity.
4. Eli Whitney's cotton gin actually increased the need for slaves, as 2/3 of the world's cotton came from the American South by 1860.
5. Black Codes were laws limiting African American (free and slave) Constitutional rights.
6. Slavery was different from area to area. It is impossible to make generalizations about slave life. Although on many plantations, *gang labor* (large groups) persisted.

Question: What do I need to know about Texas, The Alamo, etc?

Answer: Americans had been settling in Texas before 1836. Mexico hoped the Americans would become Mexicans, but later considered the settlements a conflict. Settlers saw their rights limited, and angrily declared independence. This meant a fight. The Alamo was a former mission (religious center) which was turned into a fort by the Texans.

1. In 1836, Americans and Tejanos (Texans of Mexican dissent) were defeated at the Alamo

by the Mexican army led by President Santa Anna. All soldiers within were killed, including legendary frontiersman Davy Crockett.

2. "Remember the Alamo" was yelled at the Battle of San Jacinto a month later. There, the Americans won Texas, but...

3. ***President Jackson wouldn't take Texas into the Union because it would disrupt the free/slave state balance.***

4. In 1845, President John Tyler annexed Texas as a state. It became a slave state.

Definition: Manifest Destiny

Manifest Destiny was the belief that the United States was destined to gain all land from "sea to shining sea," or between the Atlantic and Pacific Oceans. The term was coined by John L. O'Sullivan in 1845 when he wrote about it in the *US Magazine and Democratic Review*.

Manifest Destiny

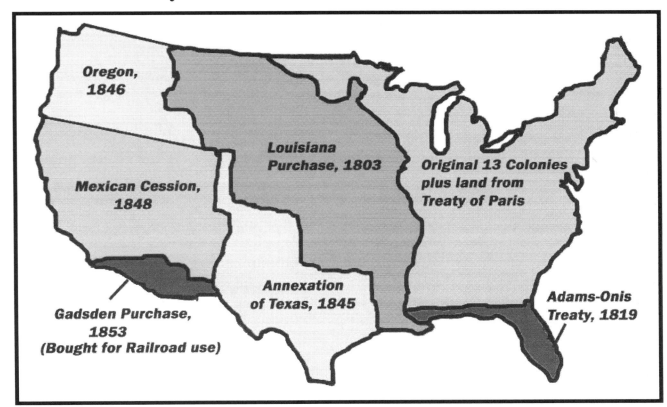

54°-40' or Fight!

In 1842, Secretary of State Daniel Webster negotiated the ***Webster-Ashburton Treaty*** with Britain. After a bloodless conflict on the Maine-Canada border called the ***Aroostook War***, this treaty decided where the border was between certain spots of the United States and British controlled Canada.

However, President James K. Polk wanted more land north of Oregon, believing that the border between the US and Canada was at the 54°-40' latitude line. Britain insisted the border was further south at 42°. Although Democrats would threaten "54°-40' or fight," negotiations in 1846 compromised the border at 49°, which is still in effect today.

Question: What do I need to know about the Mexican War, 1846-48?

Answer:

1. The United States under President Polk was itching for a fight. They wanted territory, and believed that the border between Mexico and the US was the Rio Grande. Mexico held that the border was at the Nueces River.

2. Polk and Congress were convinced that the Mexican Army "shed American blood on American soil," so a war was fought and the United States won. Future US President Zachary Taylor was a military leader in this war (hero of the Battle of Buena Vista). Note: A little-known Whig named Abraham Lincoln doubted the spot where American blood was shed.

3. The US received California and a lot of western territory after the Treaty of Guadalupe Hidalgo was ratified in 1848.

4. The new land created a potential imbalance between slave and free states, and led Ralph Waldo Emerson to say that, "Mexico will poison us!"

Definition: Wilmot Proviso, 1846

This was a failed attempt to prevent slavery from expanding into any territories taken over during the Mexican War. David Wilmot was a young Congressman whose bold idea would cause a split between Northern and Southern Democrats. In addition, a *third party* opposed to the expansion of slavery in the west was formed, called the *Free-Soil Party*. But again, Wilmot's idea never became law.

Definition: Compromise of 1850

This was Major Slave Legislation #2 of 3. Henry Clay constructed the compromise with the help of Stephen Douglas. The goal was to keep a balance between slave and free states. It failed at first as an omnibus (group of laws), but then passed as individual laws.

1. California needed to become a state after the Gold Rush of 1849. It became a free state.

2. The slave *trade* was abolished (the sale of slaves, not the institution of slavery) in the District of Columbia.

3. The Territories of New Mexico and Utah were organized under *popular sovereignty* (where the people can vote on if they want slavery or not).

4. The Fugitive Slave Act was passed, requiring all US citizens to assist in the return of runaway slaves.

5. Texas gave up some of its western land, and received compensation of $10 million to pay off its debt.

Definition: Underground Railroad

Harriet Tubman gained fame for helping run this network of safe-houses for slaves who were looking to escape to the North and Canada. This took on increased importance after the Fugitive Slave Act became law.

Definition: Ostend Manifesto, 1854

Named for a secret meeting in Ostend, Belgium, it was a scheme for the United States to purchase Cuba from Spain for $120 million. Inevitably, Cuba would have become a Southern slave state. When free-soilers (term for those who didn't want slavery to expand) in the North learned of this, they greatly protested and the plan was dropped.

Definition: Kansas-Nebraska Act, 1854

This was Major Slave Legislation #3 of 3. This law was constructed by the "Little Giant," Stephen Douglas (Clay had died by then). Originally, Congress was looking to open up land for settlement, as well as construction of a

Slavery Legislation and Compromises, 1820-1854

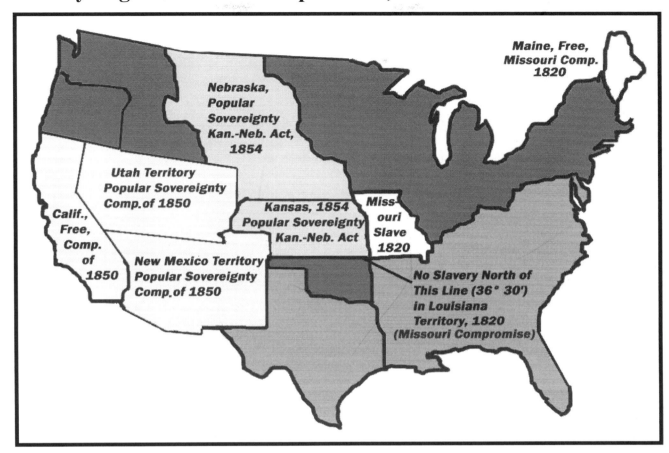

transcontinental railroad. But slavery became the issue. The Act:

1. Reversed the Missouri Compromise.

2. Let the people of Kansas and Nebraska vote on whether or not they wanted to be a slave or free state. Again, that notion is called *popular sovereignty*.

So, the three major slave legislations were: Missouri Compromise of 1820, Compromise of 1850, and the Kansas-Nebraska Act of 1854. See map above.

Definition: Bleeding Kansas

Now that popular sovereignty was law, violent pro-slavery Border Ruffians clashed with Free-Staters (some were referred to as *jay-hawkers*). Both converged on Kansas to stuff the ballot box in the slave or no slave vote. The result was massive violence. Bleeding Kansas:

1. Led to millions of dollars in property damage, and dozens dead.

2. Proved to be a mini-Civil War in Kansas.

3. John Brown became a national figure after he killed Border Ruffians at Pottawattamie, Kansas.

Definition: Lecompton Constitution

Kansas ultimately voted for slavery and it was written into the Lecompton Constitution. This new state constitution was approved by President James Buchanan.

Definition: Republican Party

With sectionalism boiling over on the slave issue, a new political party emerged. The Republican Party combined Northern Democrats, Free-Soilers, Know Nothings (anti-immigrant party), and former Whigs. Their main goal was to stop the spread of slavery in the west. Some in the party were abolitionists (against slavery altogether). Thus, the political party illustration that appears on page 27 is now complete.

Question: What abolitionist writings should I know?

Answer: Abolitionism means anti-slavery. From 1836-1845, *"gag rule"* made it impossible to petition for the abolition of slavery in the House of Representatives. However, that did not affect writers. You need to know:

1. From 1831-1865, William Lloyd Garrison published *The Liberator*, an anti-slavery newspaper. Founder of the *American Anti-Slavery Society*, he was not for total equality, but was an abolitionist. Garrison was ahead of his time, although not well received in the North at first. You should also know that he favored increasing rights for women.

2. *The Slave Narrative of Frederick Douglass*, 1845. Douglass was a free black who detailed his experience as a slave.

3. *Uncle Tom's Cabin* by Harriet Beecher Stowe, 1852. Stowe, the daughter of an abolitionist, wrote this book that detailed the horrors of slavery. In 1862, Abraham Lincoln said to her, "So you're the little woman who wrote the book that made this great war."

4. *The Impending Crisis of the South* by Hinton Rowan Helper, 1857. Written by a Southerner, this book criticized slavery, and was banned in the South.

5. The Grimké Sisters were early women reformers. In 1836, *Angelina Grimké* wrote *An Appeal to the Christian Women of the South*, in which she encouraged women to join the abolitionist cause.

6. Not a total abolitionist group, but you need to know the *American Colonization Society*. It looked to return slaves to Africa, or the colony of Liberia. It was supported by people who ranged from Northern abolitionists to Southerners nervous about the presence of free blacks.

Definition: Bleeding Sumner, 1856

Republican Charles Sumner of Massachusetts verbally attacked South Carolina Senator Andrew Butler in a speech, "The Crime Against Kansas." In response, Butler's relative, Preston Brooks, beat Sumner over the head with a cane on the Senate floor. Things got so tense in Congress that legislators carried firearms with them to the chambers each day.

Definition: *Dred Scott v. Sandford*, 1857

Dred Scott was a slave who was taken to live in free northern territory. Because he lived on free soil for an extended period of time, he believed he had legal recourse to sue for his freedom. Chief Justice Roger B. Taney (pronounced Taw´-ny), on behalf of the Supreme Court, stated that:

1. Scott was a slave, which meant that he was not protected by the United States Constitution, and couldn't even sue in court.

2. Slave compromises, specifically the Missouri Compromise, were unconstitutional, as according to the Fifth Amendment, people could not be deprived of their property. Slaves were property.

Definition: Lincoln-Douglas Debates, 1858

This refers to the Illinois Senatorial debates between Republican Abraham Lincoln and Democrat Stephen Douglas. Although he lost the election, Lincoln became a national celebrity and a critic of slavery. ***Lincoln was against the spread of slavery, but was not an abolitionist in 1858.***

In his ***Freeport Doctrine***, Douglas favored popular sovereignty over the *Dred Scott* Decision.

Definition: John Brown/Harper's Ferry, 1859

This was a raid on the federal arsenal in Harper's Ferry, Virginia (today West Virginia). Brown and a few followers attempted to fuel a larger slave revolution. It didn't happen. Brown got holed up in a firehouse, and was later captured by the Federal Army. After being hanged, he was hailed as a martyr in the North, and a terrorist in the South. Other slave rebellions to know:

Stono Rebellion, 1740 - Armed resistance in South Carolina that led to slaves losing their rights (explained in greater detail on pg. 7).

Denmark Vesey, 1822 - Failed plot in South Carolina, Vesey and others were executed.

Nat Turner, 1831 - A violent rebellion in Virginia that led to almost 200 deaths (black and white). Turner and others were executed.

Definition: Presidential Election of 1860

Two years after his defeat in the Senatorial Election of 1858, Republican Abraham Lincoln won the Presidential Election without receiving a majority of the popular vote. He received 40%. John Breckinridge, a Southern Democrat got 29%. John Bell of the Constitutional Union party received 18%, and Stephen Douglas, the Northern Democrat in the race, secured only 13%. Lincoln won the Electoral College vote with 180.

Definition: Secession

Secession occurs when states leave the Union (United States). Eleven Southern states left after the Republicans gained control of the White House. South Carolina was the first to leave, followed by the rest of the ***Confederacy***.

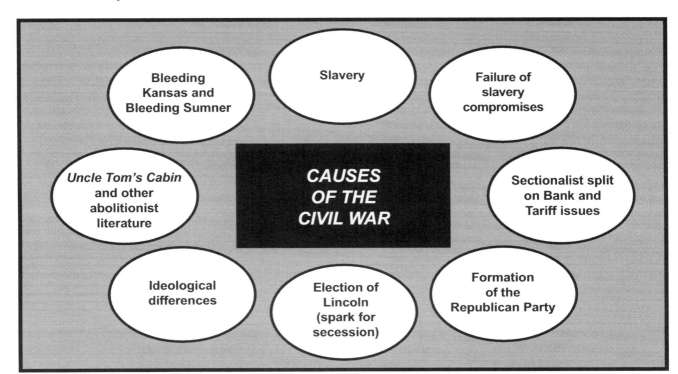

Question: So in simplest terms, what were the causes of the Civil War?

Answer:

Long Term Causes:

    1. Slavery.

    2. Sectional differences such as the bank, tariff, and economic lifestyles.

    3. Creation of the Republican Party.

    4. Ideological differences of opinion socially and politically.

    5. Failure of the slave compromises.

Immediate Cause for Secession:

The election of Lincoln in 1860, and the Republican Party controlling the White House. Secession began on December 20, 1860.

Review Questions

1. Which of the following was a provision of the Missouri Compromise of 1820?
   A) Missouri would be a free state
   B) Maine would be a slave state
   C) No slavery would exist west of the Mississippi River
   D) Western states would use popular sovereignty to determine if slavery would exist
   E) No slavery could exist in the Louisiana Territory north of the 36° 30' line

2. Which of the following best categorizes the demographics of slaves in the antebellum South?
   A) Most slaves lived in the border states
   B) Only a minority of the blacks in the United States were slaves by 1850
   C) A very small percentage of people owned slaves by the Civil War
   D) Slaves lived privately with their nuclear families on plantations
   E) All Northern states had abolished slavery by 1800

3. *"Wherever there is a human being, I see God-given rights inherent in that being, whatever may be the sex or complexion."*
   The above is a quote by:
   A) William Lloyd Garrison
   B) Hinton Rowan Helper
   C) John C. Calhoun
   D) Harriet Beecher Stowe
   E) Abraham Lincoln

4. In the antebellum period, the Southern economy was based on
   A) tobacco harvested by indentured servants
   B) transportation links that exported finished goods to the North
   C) unskilled labor from the first wave of immigration
   D) an immense production of cotton
   E) increased importance of sugar and rice

5. Use the map below to answer questions 5 and 6.

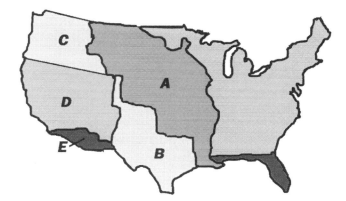

5. The issue of 54° 40' was the focus of what area?
   A) A
   B) B
   C) C
   D) D
   E) E

6. The Treaty of Guadalupe Hidalgo gave what area to the United States in 1848?
   A) A
   B) B
   C) C
   D) D
   E) E

7. The Wilmot Proviso
    A) advocated the spread of slavery
    B) created the first challenge to slavery in the Louisiana Territory
    C) abolished slavery north of the 36° 30' line
    D) was a failed attempt to prevent slavery from spreading to lands gained from Mexico
    E) became law by 1848 after the Treaty of Guadalupe Hidalgo

8. All of the following were provisions of the Compromise of 1850 EXCEPT:
    A) An end to the slave trade in Washington, DC
    B) Popular sovereignty to decide if slavery should be kept in Kansas
    C) A strict fugitive slave act
    D) Territorial changes to Texas
    E) California would be admitted as a free state

9. What was the Supreme Court's decision in the *Dred Scott v. Sandford* case?
    A) Scott was free because he lived in the area declared slave-free by the Northwest Ordinance
    B) Slave owners could not be deprived of slave property
    C) Popular sovereignty was ruled to be democratic in western states
    D) Slaves were permitted to sue in court only if they were accompanied by a slave-owner
    E) Slaves were to be given the same due process of law as other American citizens

10. What was Abraham Lincoln's stance on slavery in 1860?
    A) He thought that slavery should be abolished
    B) As a critic of slavery, he believed that slavery should not expand
    C) He preached that slaves should be denied the rights of due process
    D) He was outspoken for the need for a stronger fugitive slave act
    E) He petitioned Congress for the emancipation of only Southern slaves

Answers and Explanations

1. **E**. Henry Clay got the credit for the compromise that brought Missouri into the Union as a slave state, made Maine a free state, and outlawed slavery in the Louisiana Purchase north of the 36° 30' latitude line.

2. **C**. Contrary to common belief, only a tiny percentage of people in the antebellum South owned slaves. Most of the people were poor yeoman farmers.

3. **A**. William Lloyd Garrison did not believe in total equality for all, but was against abolition, and was for women gaining some rights.

4. **D**. After the invention of Eli Whitney's cotton gin, slavery increased in the South as cotton was easier to harvest. About 2/3 of the world's cotton was produced in the American South by 1860.

5. **C**. This is the Oregon Territory which was the focus of a land dispute between President James K. Polk and Britain.

6. **D**. This large area was land that was acquired in the Mexican War. The big question would become: should this land be slave or free?

7. **D**. David Wilmot's Proviso was made before land was officially secured in the Mexican War. He wanted to keep slavery out of all new territories acquired.

8. **B**. Popular sovereignty for Kansas and Nebraska came in 1854 with the Kansas-Nebraska Act.

9. **B**. Justice Roger B. Taney held the opinion that the government could not deprive anyone of slaves, as that would be a violation of the Fifth Amendment. Therefore, the Missouri Compromise was unconstitutional.

10. **B**. Lincoln was not an abolitionist in 1860. As a Republican candidate, he was against slavery expanding to new parts of the country.

The Civil War, 1861-1865

The turning point in American History was the Civil War. Outside of only certain major battles, you need to know about the Emancipation Proclamation, the draft, social movements, the Union and Confederate economy, and the actions of slaves and black soldiers during the war.

HERE IS WHAT YOU NEED TO KNOW:
Definition: Fort Sumter, 1861

The South attacked first to start the Civil War on April 12, 1861. Ironically, no one was killed in this initial bombardment near Charleston, South Carolina. Two people died the next day in the cannon salute to the fort. A horse died as well.

Question: Who exactly was fighting whom in the Civil War?

Answer:

North = The Union. President Lincoln. Blue uniforms. Major force was the Army of the Potomac (which had multiple leaders, ending with Ulysses S. Grant).

South = The Confederacy. President Jefferson Davis. Gray uniforms. Major force was the Army of Northern Virginia led by Robert E. Lee.

The North had the advantage, as they boasted a larger population, a stronger navy, greater farm acreage, more bank deposits, superior industry, and a greater amount of railroad track.

Question: What was Lincoln's game plan at the beginning of the Civil War?

Answer:

1. Lincoln was *not* fighting to end slavery in 1861. That changed later. In 1861, he was fighting to *maintain the Union*.

2. He wanted to secure the border states, and stop the Confederacy from expanding even further northward.

Definition: Peninsula Campaign

This was the initial war strategy for the North. The Peninsula Campaign aimed to follow the peninsula of Virginia and capture Richmond (the Confederate capital).

Definition: Anaconda Plan and Economies

The longer the war went on, the better it was for the North. Because the South had a lot of cotton to export, they needed to get to Europe to trade. Therefore, the North placed its navy around Southern ports and enforced a *blockade* of all Southern goods coming in and out of the Confederacy. The idea was to strangle the South like an anaconda (big snake) would squeeze its prey. By the end of the war, there was massive inflation and a shortage of common goods in the Confederacy. The North also experienced inflation, however not as bad, as billions of dollars in *greenbacks* (paper money) were put into circulation. Paper money causes inflation (soft money).

Note: The most famous battle of ironclad ships was between the *Monitor* (Union) and the *Merrimack* (Confederacy; also called the *Virginia*). The *Merrimack* was attempting to break the blockade. The battle ended in a draw.

Question: What major battles in the East do I need to know about *before* Gettysburg?

Answer:

1. Bull Run/Manassas Junction, 1861 (the latter is the Confederate name) - First big battle, and place where Stonewall Jackson received his nickname. The Union lost when they couldn't retreat on a road congested with picnic wagons driven by war-spectators.

2. Antietam/Sharpsburg, 1862 - Bloodiest single day in American History with over

23,000 casualties. Lee couldn't move northward through Maryland. No one won, but the Union claimed victory and issued the Emancipation Proclamation (discussed later).

3. It's important to note that in the eastern theater of the war, the Union lost almost every major battle, including at Fredericksburg and Chancellorsville.

Definition: Emancipation Proclamation

The proclamation was issued by Abraham Lincoln after Antietam in 1862, and went into effect on January 1, 1863. It:

1. Freed the slaves in the rebelling states (the states who wouldn't listen to the Union anyway). Therefore, the Proclamation...

2. Freed 0 slaves!

3. Changed the war aim from "maintaining the Union" to "freeing the slaves."

4. Kept Britain out of the war. Britain had strong ties to the South because of the cotton trade. However, now they could not support the Confederacy, as the British had abolished slavery decades before. Early in the war, in the *Trent Affair*, Confederates were captured attempting to negotiate an alliance with the British. A year later, there was controversy over the *Laird Rams*, which were ironclad ships being built in Britain for the Confederacy.

Question: What do I need to know about African American troops?

Answer:

1. At first, slaves were acquired as "contraband" and used by the army for labor.

2. The first official black regiment recognized by the Union Army was the 54th Massachusetts Volunteer Infantry (as seen in the movie *Glory*) There were earlier unofficial black troops.

3. African American soldiers were paid a lower salary than white soldiers for most of the war.

4. About 180,000 black soldiers comprised about 10% of the army by the end of the Civil War.

5. Even the Confederacy had plans for black regiments by 1865.

Definition: Gettysburg and Pickett's Charge

Lee and the Confederacy went as far north as Pennsylvania. Venturing for shoes, they wound up in Gettysburg. In the three day battle (July 1-3, 1863):

1. The Union won, and it was the turning point of the Civil War.

2. George Pickett of the Confederacy led a losing charge across an open field.

3. There were more casualties in the three days at Gettysburg than any other Civil War battle.

4. In November of 1863, Lincoln delivered the *Gettysburg Address* at the battlefield, in which he spoke about freedom, equality, uniting the country, and the sacrifices made by the soldiers. He began the speech, "Four score and seven years ago," alluding to the Declaration of Independence of 1776.

Definition: Copperheads

The Copperheads were Peace Democrats in the North and Midwest who were pro-Union, but against the Civil War. They wore pennies on their lapels in Congress, and were compared to the poisonous snake by their opponents. Clement Vallandigham was a vocal leader. Lincoln *suspended habeas corpus* and had him deported during the war. It is constitutional for a President to do so during a conflict.

Definition: New York City Draft Riots

The Enrollment Act of 1863 meant that for the first time in history, the United States could draft troops. New York City was a Democratic stronghold where there was immense opposition to the act because:

1. The draft law favored the rich. The act said that one could pay $300, or find a substitute, to get out of the draft (that was a huge amount of money). The common slogan was, "a rich man's war, poor man's fight."

2. There was racial conflict between Irish and African American populations, as they competed for the same jobs and housing in New York City. The Emancipation Proclamation meant that New York's Irish troops would be fighting for African American slaves.

3. There was both anti-war and anti-Republican sentiment in Democratic New York City.

The riot erupted in July, 1863, and led to violence against poor and affluent African Americans, Republican supporters, and rich whites. It should be noted that the South also instituted a draft with the passage of the Conscription Act of 1862. Furnishing 20 slaves would get one out of the Southern draft.

Definition: Election of 1864

Lincoln defeated Democrat George B. McClellan (whom he had fired as Commander of the Army of the Potomac). Lincoln chose Andrew Johnson, a pro-Union Southern Democrat from Tennessee as his running mate to attract Democratic votes in the North and Border States. This decision would later cause much conflict during the Reconstruction Era. Lincoln's campaign slogan was, "Don't swap horses in the middle of the river."

Definition: Total War

War used to be an event where armies would converge on a battlefield. The Civil War changed that. William Tecumseh Sherman waged war on every aspect of society, including civilians and their property. He marched his soldiers from Atlanta to Savannah in 1864 and burned everything in between.

Question: What do I need to know about the Civil War in the West?

Answer: The Union had a little more success in the West. You should know:

1. Battle of Shiloh, 1862 - Saw the Union win on the second day. It gave prominence to the then little-known Ulysses S. Grant.

2. Battle of New Orleans, 1862 - Led by Admiral David Farragut, the Union won an important naval battle.

3. Siege of Vicksburg, 1863 - The Union won, and divided the Confederacy in half by controlling the Mississippi River.

Question: What do I need to know about the Civil War *after* Gettysburg?

Answer:

1. Grant took over command of the Army of the Potomac.

2. Between 1864 to 1865, he chased Lee through Virginia, fighting at the Battle of the Wilderness, Spotsylvania Courthouse, Petersburg, and ultimately...

3. Lee surrendered to Grant at Appomattox Courthouse (that's the name of the town) on April 9, 1865.

4. There were generous terms of surrender, and Lee's army returned home. The war ended with over 600,000 lives lost.

Question: What were some of the innovations of the Civil War?

Answer: As the first "modern war," the Civil War saw many new innovations in battle, including:

1. Trench warfare, which became more prevalent after Gettysburg, was commonplace during World War I.

2. The biggest man-made explosion in the US to its day at the Battle of the Crater at Petersburg, Virginia (Union troops detonated an underground mine).

3. Ironclad ships. These were ships that had metallic sides to them.

4. Great improvements in submarine and torpedo technology.

5. Use of telegraph for communications.

Definition: John Wilkes Booth

Booth assassinated Abraham Lincoln on April 14, 1865 as part of a larger conspiracy to target members of government. He shot Lincoln at Ford's Theater during a production of *Our American Cousin*. He waited for the part of the show with the loudest laughter, pulled the trigger, and then leaped to the stage, breaking his leg in the process. Yet he managed to escape (he was captured twelve days later). Andrew Johnson became President when Lincoln died the next day.

After the Civil War came the difficult task of rebuilding the South. The Presidents wanted lenient Reconstruction that would peacefully bring Southern states back into the union. The Radical Republican Congress wanted harsh Reconstruction that punished the South and gave immediate constitutional rights to the newly freed slaves. Although Reconstruction laws provided basic civil rights, the enforcement of such legislation would be nearly impossible. After the federal government pulled out its troops, it would be nearly 100 years before African Americans received similar civil rights.

Reconstruction, 1865-1877

Definition: Reconstruction

1865-1877 was a time period where the following had to be addressed:

1. The South's infrastructure had to be rebuilt.
2. African Americans needed to be given Constitutional rights.
3. The Southern states had to be readmitted into the Union and agree to follow the Constitution.

Question: What was the difference between Presidential and Congressional (Radical) Reconstruction?

Answer: Presidential Reconstruction (from about 1865-1867) was lenient. Democratic President Andrew Johnson did not want to punish the South. He vetoed much Congressional legislation, and offered pardons to former Confederates. Note: Lincoln also wanted to be lenient, and treat Reconstruction as if the South had never seceded. But, John Wilkes Booth took away any hopes of Lincoln bringing peace.

Radical Reconstruction began by 1867. It was harsher and involved military troops enforcing laws in the South.

Definition: 10% Plan/Wade Davis Bill

Presidential Reconstruction favored a 10% plan. This meant that a state could re-enter the Union after 10% of its voting citizens (from 1860) agreed to take a loyalty oath to the United States Constitution.

Congress favored the Wade-Davis Bill which stipulated a 50% plan. Before the assassination, Lincoln pocket-vetoed this bill (did not sign it, and it automatically became a veto).

Question: What Reconstruction Amendments do I need to know?

Answer:
Thirteenth - Abolition of slavery, 1865.

Fourteenth - Equality of citizenship for males, plus a due process clause for the states, 1868. Note: Native Americans were not included.

Fifteenth - Universal male suffrage (voting), 1870.

Definition: Black Codes

Black Codes appear at various times in history. They existed in the South during early Reconstruction, and denied free blacks Constitutional rights such as freedom of speech and the right to serve on juries. Southern whites feared that if free blacks had rights, they would feel empowered to dismantle the Southern plantation system. Radical Republicans looked to end these unfair codes.

Definition: Radical Republicans

Congressman *Thaddeus Stevens* and Senator *Charles Sumner* were the two most famous Radical Republicans. The Radical Republicans controlled Reconstruction by 1867, and hoped to bring basic rights and freedoms to former slaves. They also wanted to use force to make Reconstruction a harsh reality for the South.

Definition: Freedmen's Bureau

Established in 1865, the Freedmen's Bureau looked to adjust newly-freed blacks to Southern society. The organization aimed to help with housing, education, food, healthcare, and jobs. President Johnson later vetoed a bill in 1866 that would have increased the Bureau's power.

Definition: Civil Rights Act of 1866

Passed over President Johnson's veto, this act hoped to make African Americans equal under the law. However, the law was not enforced very well. The Civil Rights Era, one hundred years later, looked to deliver a more thorough equality.

Definition: Reconstruction Acts of 1867

These were very important components to Reconstruction legislation. Passed over Johnson's vetoes, the acts:

1. Divided the South into 5 districts occupied by Union troops.

2. Forced all former Confederate states to ratify the Fourteenth Amendment.

3. Made the former Confederate states create new state constitutions which would ensure the voting rights of former slaves. The federal government would have to approve the new state constitutions.

The Southern states had to obey these acts to be readmitted to the Union.

Definition: Ku Klux Klan

There was uneasiness in the South because Reconstruction legislation aimed to help former slaves. The KKK began as a fraternal organization, and escalated into a terrorist one under the guidance of former Confederate General Nathan Bedford Forrest. They targeted blacks through lynching (murder, often by hanging), and other violence. The organization disbanded after the *Enforcement Act* (1870), and *Ku Klux Act* (1871). The Klan would make a comeback in the 1920s (discussed later).

Definition: Impeachment of Andrew Johnson

The Radical Republicans hated Johnson, the Democratic President. They looked for any excuse to get rid of him. That excuse came when Johnson fired the Secretary of War, Edwin M. Stanton, thereby violating the *Tenure of Office Act* (according to the law, he was supposed to consult with Congress first). The House of Representatives impeached Johnson (brought him up on charges). However, the Senate found him not guilty by one vote, and he was never removed from office. He remains one of only two Presidents ever impeached (Bill Clinton was the other).

Definition: Amnesty Act of 1872

This act permitted former Confederate leaders and secessionists to hold office again. It also allowed about 160,000 of them to vote. This helped the Democrats reclaim the South from the Republicans.

Definition: Carpetbaggers

This was the label for Northerners who went to the South for political and/or economic gain during Reconstruction. They were resented by Southerners.

Definition: Scalawags

Scalawags were Southerners loyal to the Republican Party. They often worked alongside carpetbaggers and newly-freed blacks to create new state constitutions. They were greater in number than the carpetbaggers. Remember, traditionally Southerners were Democrats.

Definition: Election of 1876

Samuel J. Tilden (Democrat) was leading Rutherford B. Hayes (Republican) in both popular and Electoral Votes. But alas...20 Electoral Votes were disputed. A 15-member Electoral Commission comprised of 5 Representatives, 5 Senators, and 5 Supreme Court Judges had to decide who would receive the votes. Ultimately, a compromise in 1877 produced the following:

1. The Republicans received all of the

Electoral Votes, which gave Hayes the Presidential Election.

2. The Democrats got removal of Union troops from the South, thus ending Reconstruction.

Definition: Home Rule

When the Republicans pulled Union troops out, it meant that the South would rule itself for the first time since the Civil War. Often, this meant not following Reconstruction legislation. This post-Reconstruction time was known as Home Rule. Home Rule pleased **Redeemers**, or those who tried to eradicate Republican influence from the South during Reconstruction. For over a century, every Southern State would vote Democratic in Presidential Elections. This was called *The Solid South*.

Definition: Sharecropping/Crop Lien

Newly-freed slaves, often working for their former masters, lived an impoverished existence as a sharecropper. Sharecropping meant farming for only a share of harvested crops, with much of the profit going to the landlord for rent. In such a "crop-lien" system, the landlord also provided supplies, but had a lien on the crops yet to be grown. Because of this, sharecroppers experienced extreme "debt peonage," or poverty. The practice continued into the twentieth century.

Definition: Jim Crow Laws

Historians believe that the term Jim Crow came from a Thomas D. Rice minstrel (sarcastic portrayal of black culture) show from the 1830s. There was no real Jim Crow.

The laws were all about "separate but equal." That meant segregating blacks from whites, assuming that their bathrooms, schools, and water fountains were equal (which of course, they weren't). After the Supreme Court upheld (agreed with) "separate but equal" in the 1896 *Plessy v. Ferguson* case, Jim Crow survived until the mid-twentieth century.

Question: After Reconstruction, how did the South prevent free blacks from voting?

Answer: To avoid the Fifteenth Amendment, Southerners used all of the following:

1. Violence at the polls. Southern whites typically voted Democratic. Surely, African Americans would vote Republican. There were no secret ballots back then, and intimidation played a part at the polls. As early as 1875, the **Mississippi Plan** organized such violence against African American voters.

2. A poll tax, or a tax to vote. Before voting, free blacks would have to present a receipt proving they paid their tax. The 24th Amendment would outlaw this practice in 1964.

3. Literacy Tests. In order to vote, one had to pass a difficult exam. Whites would not have to take it because of the...

4. Grandfather Clause. If your grandfather could vote in the Election of 1860, the literacy test would not disqualify you from voting. White's grandfathers could vote. Newly-freed blacks' grandfathers had been slaves who couldn't vote.

Definition: New South

After the Civil War, there was a movement in the South for more industry with less dependence on the plantation system. Some cities like Atlanta industrialized. Most other areas did not add significant industry.

Definition: Slaughterhouse Cases, 1873

These were cases that put into question the protections of the Fourteenth Amendment. Louisiana created a corporation for the slaughtering of livestock. This corporation put all of the local slaughterhouses out of work. The butchers who lost their jobs believed that the Louisiana creation was a violation to their Fourteenth Amendment right to exercise free trade equally. The butchers lost, as the Supreme Court stated that the Amendment did not protect citizenship from *state law*. Therefore states could create a slaughterhouse for the health and safety of the public.

Review Questions

1. The Enrollment Act of 1863
   A) allowed the Confederacy to recruit soldiers from rural areas
   B) made it illegal to pay volunteers in the Union Army
   C) allowed draftees to pay to get out of service
   D) permitted the North to confiscate slaves from the South
   E) brought forth the first African American regiments in American History

2. The 1863 battle which proved to be the turning point of the Civil War was fought at
   A) Antietam Creek
   B) Bull Run
   C) Shiloh
   D) Gettysburg
   E) Vicksburg

3. How did the Anaconda Plan affect the Confederacy's ability to wage war by 1865?
   A) Lincoln's plan made it nearly impossible for the Confederates to recruit troops
   B) By blockading the South, it was difficult for the Confederacy to maintain supplies
   C) Militarily, the Confederates were defeated by 1862
   D) By controlling the Mississippi River, the Confederacy was divided in half
   E) Slave rebellions began to expand throughout the South, disrupting the labor force

4. The Emancipation Proclamation
   A) freed slaves only in the rebelling territories
   B) led to a declaration of war by Britain on the Confederacy
   C) freed all slaves in the Union
   D) was passed after the victory at Gettysburg
   E) freed only the slaves in the North

5. Black Codes passed in first few years of Reconstruction looked to
   A) force sharecroppers back into slavery
   B) allow African Americans to write new state constitutions
   C) prevent the rights given by the Fifteenth Amendment of 1870
   D) deny basic Constitutional rights and economic endeavors to African Americans
   E) increase the presence of the Ku Klux Klan

6. Which of the following ideas was an example of Presidential Reconstruction?
   A) Wade-Davis Bill
   B) 10% Plan
   C) Reconstruction Acts of 1867
   D) Civil Rights Act of 1866
   E) Fourteenth Amendment

7. During and after Reconstruction, most blacks
   A) moved to the North to seek jobs
   B) received 40 acres and a mule to start a new life
   C) lived in constant debt peonage as sharecroppers
   D) preferred to stay in bondage with their masters
   E) moved to border states to avoid discrimination

8. Carpetbag state governments
   A) limited the rights of African Americans
   B) legislated to limit the power of the Ku Klux Klan
   C) created ways to avoid enforcing the Fifteenth Amendment
   D) were controlled by northern whites and African Americans
   E) continued to create civil rights legislation after 1877

9. In the Reconstruction period, Radical Republicans created a policy that
A) divided the South into five military districts that enforced Reconstruction legislation
B) allowed all former Confederates to make their own state constitutions without the help of freedmen
C) lowered tariffs on all foreign imports
D) sent all free slaves to Liberia
E) allowed Southern states to return to the Union after 60% of voters took a loyalty oath

10. Why did Reconstruction end in 1877?
A) The Fourteenth Amendment was finally ratified
B) A victorious KKK ended military rule
C) The Reconstruction Acts of 1867 had been declared unconstitutional by a unanimous Supreme Court
D) The Election of 1876 led to a compromise ending Reconstruction
E) All of the state constitutions had been written and ratified, so Reconstruction was no longer necessary

Answers and Explanations

1. **C**. This act created the controversial Northern draft. The law allowed people to pay $300 to get out of conscription. Only the rich could afford that. This stipulation was mostly responsible for the 1863 New York City Draft Riot.

2. **D**. After Pickett's Charge at Gettysburg, the North had a decisive victory that turned the tide of the war.

3. **B**. Like a big snake, the North suffocated supplies from the South with a blockade.

4. **A**. The Emancipation Proclamation did not free slaves in the Northern or border states. It only freed slaves in the South, where no one obeyed federal law.

5. **D**. Black Codes were Southern laws preventing basic Constitutional Rights, such as due process in the court system. Be careful if you chose C. The Fifteenth Amendment came much later in the Reconstruction process.

6. **B**. Lincoln's plan stated that if 10% of the voting public took an oath to be loyal to the Constitution, a Southern state could return to the Union. Lincoln did not sign the Wade-Davis Bill, which would have increased the percentage to 50%.

7. **C**. Sharecropping was the economic system that kept blacks in poverty during and after Reconstruction. They worked for a share of their harvested crops. Oftentimes, freedmen worked for their former masters.

8. **D**. The Carpetbag Governments were resented by the South, as carpetbaggers were Northerners helping to create state constitutions. They did so alongside free blacks and scalawags.

9. **A**. The Reconstruction Acts of 1867 were passed by Radical Republicans as a means to militarily enforce legislation.

10. **D**. In 1877, a compromise gave Republican Rutherford B. Hayes the Presidential Election. In return, the Democrats (who made up the *Solid South*) received an end to military rule during Reconstruction.

The Gilded Age, c1870-1890

Mark Twain coined the term, "Gilded Age" to describe the time period between the 1870s-1900. Gilded meant that what appeared to be golden on the outside, was really junk on the inside. It seemed as though everything was great in this era. There were "robber barons" who grew quite rich in their monopolized industries. Some of the rich rose to power after being rather poor. But in truth, 1% of the population controlled 99% of the wealth. The laboring class was exploited both as workers and as consumers. Unions attempted to gain rights such as an 8-hour day. Despite the efforts of their strikes, the skilled and unskilled laborers never got the big piece of the pie. To complicate matters, millions of immigrants came to America to work in the factories. In response, there was much anti-immigrant sentiment (nativism).

HERE IS WHAT YOU NEED TO KNOW:
Definition: Gilded Age

Coined by Mark Twain, the term refers to the time period from the 1870s until about 1900. Gilded means gold on the outside, and junk on the inside. Life during this time period looked good in terms of industry and invention, but in truth, the common people were suffering.

Definition: Robber Barons/Trusts

The term **robber barons** was used to describe industrialists who controlled monopolies, or *trusts*, during the Gilded Age. They included Andrew Carnegie (steel), Cornelius Vanderbilt (railroads), and John D. Rockefeller (oil). Horatio Alger was known for writing *dime novels* about some of these men, like Carnegie, who went from "Rags to Riches" during the Gilded Age.

Trusts formed when one company took over the stock of competing companies in "trust" agreements. This often led to *monopolies*, where one huge corporation controlled almost the entire market. Competition fizzled and prices were often manipulated.

To control most of the steel industry, Carnegie bought out the raw materials and railroad lines associated with production. This is called *vertical integration*. He also looked to buy out similar companies, or merge with them. This is called *horizontal integration*.

Definition: The Gospel of Wealth

This was Carnegie's decree that the super-rich should be charitable and give back to society for the common good. However, a fortune should not be squandered, and must be donated to those wise enough to spend it properly.

Definition: Social Darwinism

Playing off Charles Darwin's Theory of Evolution, this was a belief in "survival of the fittest" in the business world. This notion was a defense of monopolies. Note: These same Darwinian principles would be applied decades later during the Age of Imperialism when the United States took over foreign territories.

Edward Bellamy wrote a utopian novel called *Looking Backward 2000-1887*, in which he gave a socialist look at the future. He showed how government reform movements would one day save the world from the evils of the trusts.

Question: What were the scandals of President Ulysses S. Grant's Administration?

Answer: The following scandals took place at the onset of the Gilded Age:

1. Crédit Mobilier of 1872 was a scandal

where the railroad companies and construction suppliers were owned by the same people. The supplier, Crédit Mobilier, was charging inflated prices for construction materials. The government-backed Union Pacific happily paid these prices. Of course, with inflated prices came bribes and kickbacks to the Congressmen involved.

2. The Salary Grab of 1873 was when Congress voted itself a 50% pay raise. Other salary increases were in the same bill. Grant signed this just before his second inauguration.

3. The Whiskey Ring of 1873 was a scandal in which federal whiskey taxes wound up in the pockets of distillers and politicians. Grant's Private Secretary was accused of wrongdoing.

Question: What was Boss Tweed's political machine?

Answer: William M. Tweed was the head of Tammany Hall, a *political machine* in New York City where people voted "early and often" to support the Democratic Party. Tweed's "Ring" basically ran New York City, as members of the Democratic Party controlled all powerful offices there. Tammany Hall also helped immigrants find jobs in exchange for votes. New York was an oasis of *municipal (city) corruption*, as bribery and kickbacks were common. *The New York Times* eventually exposed Tweed with the help of cartoonist Thomas Nast. After being prosecuted by attorney Samuel J. Tilden, Tweed went to prison.

Definition: Pendleton Act, 1883

After President James Garfield was assassinated by an unhappy office-seeker, this act attempted to rid the country of the spoils system (patronage system where a candidate appoints supporters to offices). The act provided for a civil service test to be taken by all government office-seekers.

Definition: Knights of Labor

The Knights of Labor was founded in 1869 as an industrial union led by *Terence Powderly*. With over 700,000 members by 1886, the union fought for an end to child labor, an 8-hour day, and equal pay for equal work. They also allowed African Americans and women to join. The Knights were quite often involved in strikes (though Powderly was against excess striking). A strike is a refusal to work.

Definition: AFL

The American Federation of Labor was founded in 1886 as a *craft union* where people of a similar craft, or job, were grouped together. Their early leader was *Samuel Gompers*. Unlike the Knights of Labor, Gompers urged striking only when necessary. He fought for "*bread and butter*" issues, like an 8-hour day, and higher wages. These were basic financial topics that affected the daily lives of the union members.

The AFL promoted *collective bargaining*, where employees met with employers to compromise and discuss differences of opinion.

Here's how you can distinguish the two major unions:

BAGS - **B**read **B**utter Issues / **A**FL /**G**ompers / **S**trike less with collective bargaining

KUPS - **K**nights / **U**nskilled / **P**owderly / **S**trike more...Unskilled spellers can't spell cups.

Definition: IWW

The Industrial Workers of the World (Wobblies) were founded a bit after the Gilded Age in 1905. At times they were led by a vocal socialist, *Eugene V. Debs*. They were the most radical of all unions, and largely comprised of new immigrants.

Definition: Molly Maguires

The "Mollies" were Irish-American coal miners in Pennsylvania who belonged to a secret society. They were charged with kidnapping and murder. With sketchy evidence, 20 of the miners were executed in 1877.

Definition: Mugwumps

During the 1880s, the Republican Party was divided. The Stalwarts (or Old Guard) were more conservative than the Half-Breeds, who favored civil service reform. But the Mugwumps were so dissatisfied with their party that they voted for Democrat Grover Cleveland against Republican James G. Blaine in the Election of 1884.

Definition: Railroad strike of 1877

1877 was the end of Reconstruction, and the beginning of the "Labor Question." The Railroad Strike, or "Great Upheaval" occurred because of a cut to wages after the Panic of 1873. Sympathy strikes (strikes in nearby areas sympathetic to the cause) spread throughout the country from West Virginia to Illinois. President Hayes broke up this strike with federal troops because it was disrupting interstate commerce and the violence was getting out of hand. Note: In the Gilded Age, Presidents tended to side with "Big Business," and not the consumer or worker.

Definition: Haymarket Affair, 1886

In Chicago, a bomb went off in Haymarket Square during a rally near the McCormick Harvesting Machine Company. Police fired weapons in response. Both cops and civilians were killed. This was a landmark event as:

1. Unions were blamed and ultimately associated with socialism and anarchy (anti-establishment).

2. Since many union members were immigrants, there was an increase in nativism, or animosity towards foreigners (nativism explained in-depth later).

3. There was a sharp decrease in unionization.

Definition: Homestead Strike, 1892

This was yet another defeat for unions. Andrew Carnegie's steel plant in Homestead, Pennsylvania began to unionize. Carnegie fought unionization, and violence occurred between strikers and Pinkerton (private) detectives. Strikers were later arrested and tried for treason.

Definition: Pullman Strike of 1894

Pullman cars were luxury railroad cars. When wages went down at the factory, the workers went on strike. Eugene V. Debs, a socialist, instructed railroad workers to halt trains with Pullman cars on them. Much violence and property damage accompanied the strike. President Grover Cleveland said that the strike actions disrupted federal mail. He got a court order (injunction) to end the strike, and Debs went to prison. This was another example of the President siding with employers.

Definition: Panic of 1893 and Coxey's Army of 1894

Every few decades of the nineteenth century (1837, 1857, 1873, and 1893) saw a financial panic. The one in 1893 led to immense unemployment. Ohio politician Jacob Coxey gathered an "army" of unemployed men who demanded that the government provide jobs in public works (government construction). Coxey marched through the country, and into Washington, DC. There, members of his "army" were arrested for trespassing on the US Capitol lawn.

Definition: Interstate Commerce Act and the Interstate Commerce Commission, 1887

The act created the Interstate Commerce

Committee that looked to ensure that railroad shipping fees were "reasonable and just." They also made sure that rates were published so price discrimination didn't happen. Of course, in the Gilded Age, nothing was what it seemed. The Gilded Age Presidents appointed pro-Railroad ICC commissioners, so little help to the consumer occurred.

Before the ICC, farmers pressured Illinois to create legislation to prevent inflated prices for hauling crops on railroads. In the 1877 case *Munn v. Illinois*, the Supreme Court protected the state government's ability to regulate the prices of private industries. The impact of this decision was greatly reduced by the 1886 *Wabash* case (*Wabash, St. Louis & Pacific Railway Company v. Illinois*). Hence, an ICC was needed to address the controversial issue of railroad pricing.

Definition: Sherman Anti-Trust Act, 1890

1. Named for legislator John Sherman, this act attempted to break up monopolies and trusts that exploited consumers.

2. The following is a very common quote: "Any contract or combination in *restraint of trade* is illegal." If you hear "restraint of trade," Sherman is your man.

3. The act did not define "restraint of trade" well, and the law was mostly used *at first to break up unions*.

Question: What Gilded Age inventions should I know about?

Answer:

1. The incandescent light bulb by Thomas Edison stayed on longer than earlier light bulbs.

2. Henry *Bessemer's Process* found a way to eliminate the impurities in pig iron so it could be mass-produced quicker.

3. In 1869, the Golden Spike was hammered at Promontory Summit, Utah. This completed the Transcontinental Railroad. Railroads were given a lot of land from the federal government, as the United States had a vested interest in linking the country together. A railroad line across the nation would encourage transportation, settlement, and trade.

4. In 1883, the Brooklyn Bridge opened in New York City. The largest steel suspension bridge of its time connected Brooklyn to Manhattan.

5. Alexander Graham Bell's telephone would revolutionize communications in the coming centuries.

Question: What were the two great waves of immigration?

Answer:

1. Old Immigration - c1845-1860 - First Great Wave. These immigrants were mostly from Western European countries such as Ireland, Britain, and Germany.

2. New Immigration - c1890-1920 - Second Great Wave. These immigrants were mostly from Southern and Eastern European countries such as Italy, Russia, and Poland.

There are two theories on immigration. The first, *the melting pot*, calls for a total assimilation (Americanization) of newcomers. In this theory, immigrants lose their culture as if they have jumped into a crucible (melting pot), thus blending with all other US citizens. The second theory is *cultural pluralism*, or the "salad bowl" idea. In this metaphor, immigrants maintain their cultural identity as they coexist with other Americans.

Question: What was nativism, and how did it affect immigrant *quotas*?

Answer:

Nativism is a fear of foreigners based on nationalistic feelings. Nativism existed during the first Great Wave of Immigration, as the

Know Nothing Party was founded because of anti-Irish-Catholic sentiment. Later in the century, Nativism led to:

1. The Chinese Exclusion Act of 1882 which limited Chinese immigration.

2. The Gentlemen's Agreement of 1907 in which Japan agreed to limit emigration to the United States. **Commodore Matthew Perry** opened up Japan to westernization in the 1850s. After modernizing their economy, many immigrated to the US, but faced segregation and discrimination.

3. The *Quota Acts* of the 1920s (specifically the Emergency Quota Act of 1921 and the National Origins Act of 1924) set limits on immigration, especially from Southern and Eastern Europe. This meant that government policy favored the more assimilated (Americanized) immigrants from Western European nations such as Britain. Immigration from Eastern Europe was greatly curtailed.

The quota acts were inspired by a belief in a pseudoscience called *eugenics*. Eugenics attempted to rank the races. On intelligence and desirability, Southern and Eastern European immigrants were ranked lower than Western Europeans.

The West, 1860-1890

In the West, the glory of "free land" led to the rise of lawless towns. In addition, America continued to expand at the expense of Native American populations. Wounded Knee became the Trail of Tears for a new generation.

HERE IS WHAT YOU NEED TO KNOW:
Definition: Homestead Act of 1862

Passed during the Civil War, this act provided public land for private use. "Free Land" became the slogan, as about 270 million acres (10% of the US) were claimed and settled under this act. A homestead typically was 160 acres in size.

Definition: Transcontinental Railroad

This was a railroad that linked the entire country together. The Central Pacific (with the help of Chinese immigrants) built east from Sacramento, California. The Union Pacific built west from Council Bluffs, Iowa. The Golden Spike was hammered at Promontory Summit, Utah on May 10, 1869.

As mentioned earlier, the government provided land to railroad companies in support of this project. The railroads led to the development of cities in the west and created new demands for meat. This caused an expansion of the longhorn cattle industry which was based in Texas. Cowboys herded the cattle to their final destinations.

Question: What famous gunslingers should I know about in the Wild West?

Answer: With western land being claimed so fast, there was little time for the government to provide law enforcement. In case you receive an essay on the west, you might want to throw in…

Billy The Kid - The head of the *Regulators* in the West, he shot a sheriff, escaped a death sentence, and then died on the run.

Jesse James - Part of the *James-Younger Gang*, and a former member of Quantrill's Raiders (Confederate guerilla warfare soldiers). He robbed stagecoaches and banks. He was shot by a former partner in crime, Robert Ford.

Annie Oakley - Part of *Buffalo Bill Cody's Wild West Show*, she had one of the best shots in the wild west, and performed for thousands.

Wild Bill Hickok - A legendary gunslinger of the Old West, he was shot playing poker while holding Aces and Eights…The Dead Man's Hand.

Wyatt Earp - He made a fortune playing faro (a gambling game of number prediction) in the Old West. Later, he became a man of law. He was triumphant in the legendary gunfight at the OK Corral in Tombstone, Arizona where outlaw Billy Clanton was killed.

Definition: Dawes Severalty Act of 1887

The goal of this act was to assimilate Native Americans rather than remove them to reservations. The government granted plots of land and United States citizenship to Native Americans who, "adopted the habits of civilized life." This program was mostly a failure because the best land was typically saved for whites, and the government would not give full control of the land until 25 years after its issuance.

Definition: Buffalo (Bison) Depletion

Buffalo were vital for Native American survival on the western plains. In 1870 there were about 13 million grazing there. By 1883, there were only a few hundred left. Buffalo hunters, like Buffalo Bill Cody, were celebrated as American heroes. Trains offered voyages where people could blast guns at the animals from the sides of railroad cars. This left a trail of carcasses littering the Great Plains.

Definition: Little Big Horn, 1876

This was the location of General George Custer's "Last Stand." After gold was reportedly spotted in the Black Hills of Montana, the army went to inspect. Six tribes outnumbered the American forces, and killed everyone including Custer. The battle increased Native American morale, and angered the US Government.

Definition: Ghost Dance and Wounded Knee, 1890

In the Dakotas, the Sioux Indians put on Ghost Shirts that they thought would make them invincible to bullets. Following the prophet *Wovoka*, they believed that by doing a dance, they would rid the Dakotas of white expansionists, and bring about peace. However, in the midst of the movement, the US Cavalry showed up near Wounded Knee Creek, SD. In a chaotic and frantic exchange, over 150 Native Americans, including Sioux leader Sitting Bull, were killed. The Wounded Knee Massacre became a symbol of Native American discrimination, and oppression.

Definition: Helen Hunt Jackson

In 1881 Jackson wrote *A Century of Dishonor*, a nonfiction work that detailed the horrors of Native American Removal in the nineteenth century. She documented how thousands of Native Americans were pushed from the eastern US to the west, and their lack of Constitutional protections.

Definition: Turner Thesis

After the closing of the American frontier, Harvard professor Frederick Jackson Turner wrote a thesis in 1893 concluding that the West (frontier) personified the story of America. He displayed the importance of how the frontier line had always sparked individual strength and democracy. He believed that the West was the most important component of the American story.

Also, the frontier offered a "safety valve," meaning free land promised opportunity which diffused economic and social conflict. Adversaries of the thesis believe that Turner overemphasized the importance of the frontier, as other issues such as slavery and industrialization proved to be much larger stories.

Review Questions

1. Boss Tweed was most associated with
   A) muckraking
   B) abolition
   C) political machine politics
   D) trustbusting
   E) Radical Republicanism

2. The Chicago Haymarket Affair of 1886
   A) was organized by Samuel Gompers
   B) ultimately led to a decrease in union membership
   C) was broken up by President Cleveland
   D) displayed the discontent of farmers
   E) occurred during Reconstruction

3. Robber barons of the late nineteenth century tried to
   A) use newspapers and media to exploit the perils of society
   B) eliminate competition in their particular industries
   C) increase the number of members in industrial unions
   D) conquer territories in the west
   E) use political machines to increase Democratic votes in urban areas

4. "Bread and Butter" issues are most associated with what union?
   A) American Federation of Labor
   B) Knights of Labor
   C) Industrial Workers of the World
   D) International Ladies' Garment Workers' Union
   E) Congress of Industrial Organization

5. A purpose of the Interstate Commerce Act of 1887 was to
   A) make all food and drugs safe to consume
   B) prevent illegal procedure in intrastate trade
   C) end unfair practices of the railroads
   D) prevent unsafe working conditions in factories
   E) put an end to each state taxing imports from other states

6. *"Every contract, combination in the form of trust or otherwise, or conspiracy, in restraint of trade or commerce among the several States, or with foreign nations, is declared to be illegal."*
   The above quote can be found in the
   A) Dawes Act
   B) Interstate Commerce Act
   C) Elastic Clause
   D) Reconstruction Acts of 1867
   E) Sherman Anti-Trust Act

7. The Dawes Severalty Act of 1887 wanted to
   A) expand voting rights to Native Americans so low populated areas could sustain a strong electorate
   B) alleviate the feelings of discontent amongst Native Americans after the Wounded Knee massacre
   C) move all Native Americans west of the Mississippi River onto reservations
   D) assimilate Native Americans by offering the promise of land and rights
   E) decrease the amount of land Native Americans could own in common with their ancestors

8. Frederick Jackson Turner's thesis sought to
   A) illustrate the importance of the West in United States History
   B) detail the hardships of migrant farm workers
   C) increase unionization in the United States
   D) break up trusts in corporate America
   E) bring attention to the plight of Native Americans

9. New Immigrants (1890-1920) mostly came from
   A) Southern and Eastern Europe
   B) Western Europe
   C) South America
   D) Asia
   E) Canada and Mexico

10. Why was there *most likely* an increase in nativism towards new immigrants 1890-1920?
   A) Irish immigrants began to take jobs away from established Americans
   B) Russian immigrants took white collar and medical jobs away from physicians
   C) New immigrants were different in culture, and did not assimilate as well as "old immigrants"
   D) Skilled jobs were being taken by new immigrants
   E) German immigrants did not speak the same dialect of English as their predecessors

Answers and Explanations

1. **C**. William Tweed was the leader of the Tammany Hall political machine in New York City. Its goal was to churn out votes for the Democratic Party. Tweed embezzled a great deal of money in the process, and his "Ring" controlled the city of New York.

2. **B**. After a bomb went off in Chicago's Haymarket Square, anarchist immigrants were blamed. This led to a fear of immigrants, and the unions they were a part of. Union membership declined.

3. **B**. By eliminating their competition, robber barons hoped to monopolize their industry.

4. **A**. Samuel Gompers and the American Federation of Labor believed in basic financial topics that affected everyday life. Some "bread and butter" issues included higher wages and an 8-hour work day.

5. **C**. The Interstate Commerce Act created the Interstate Commerce Commission that looked to end unfair railroad activities. Watch out for choice B. In*tra*state means within one state.

6. **E**. "Restraint of trade" is from the Sherman Anti-Trust Act. But be warned! At first the act was used to break up unions instead of trusts.

7. **D**. The Dawes Act offered land and citizenship in exchange for assimilation. The act failed, as whites still claimed the best land. Also, a 25-year period would need to elapse before the land was owned for good.

8. **A**. Turner's Thesis stated that the west exemplified the story of America.

9. **A**. Old Immigrants came from Western Europe. New Immigrants came from Southern and Eastern Europe.

10. **C**. New Immigrants were not as well accepted, as they had a culture quite different from "older immigrants" from Western Europe. The Western Europeans assimilated more easily because of their similarities to American culture and language.

Populism and The Progressive Era, c1892-1920

The Gilded Age alienated the common American. Populism was a movement started by farmers to bring the government back to the people. Although they never elected a President, some of their ideas became a reality during the Progressive Era. The Progressives brought about immense change to the social, political, and economic lives of the American people. New amendments, aid to immigrants, direct participation in politics, and regulation of business were just some of their many reforms. The Progressive Era weakened after World War I when fears of communism swept the nation.

HERE IS WHAT YOU NEED TO KNOW:
Definition: Granger Movement and Farmers' Alliance

Both movements were predecessors to Populism. *The National Grange of the Order of Patrons of Husbandry* defended farmers against big business. The *Farmers' Alliance* organized farmers economically and politically.

Definition: Populist Party

Also known as the People's Party, they were a short-lived political party comprised mostly of farmers. In 1892, they drafted their platform at Omaha, Nebraska (Omaha Platform) and ran James Weaver for President. He lost.

Question: What did the Populists want?

Answer: Mnemonic Device - **STAR 16**

S - **S**enators to be directly elected.

T - Graduated/Progressive Income **T**ax (the more you make, the more they take).

A - **A**ustralian Ballot (secret ballot).

R - Regulation of the **R**ailroads by the government.

16 - Coinage of silver at a ratio of **16**:1 with gold.

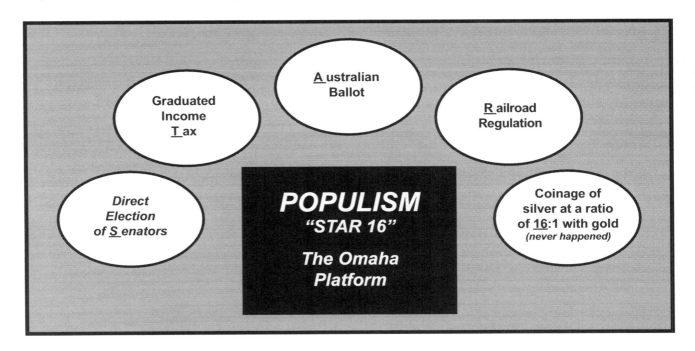

Question: Why did the Populists care so much about the silver issue?

Answer: By 1892, the prices of crops were falling...drastically. So, to make money, farmers **grew more crops!** But when you grow more crops, there's greater supply than demand and...**they lose their value!** So now you have to...*grow even more crops!* This vicious cycle of overproduction and deflation of prices put farmers out of business. They couldn't pay their mortgages. However, since mortgages are on a fixed rate, if more silver was put into circulation instead of gold, *inflation* would occur. That's because silver is worth less than gold. This would increase the prices of the farm goods, and make that fixed mortgage easier to pay off.

This is very similar to the hard money/soft money battle of the Jacksonian Era (see pg. 34). Flooding the market with silver has the same result as printing more paper money - inflation.

Question: Of what the Populists wanted, what eventually became law?

Answer: Don't underestimate the importance of third parties in American History. They bring attention to new issues. Here is the Populist success rate:

S - Senators to be directly elected...***Became the Seventeenth Amendment (1913)***

T - Graduated/Progressive Income **T**ax... ***Became the Sixteenth Amendment (1913)***

A - Australian Ballot...***Became Law c1900***

R - Regulation of the **R**ailroads by the government...***Became law c1900***

16 - Coinage of silver at a ratio of **16**:1 with gold...**Never happened**. *But to the farmers it was the most important aspect of the Omaha Platform.*

Definition: William Jennings Bryan

Dashing and handsome in 1896, Bryan received the nomination for President from both the Democrats and the Populists. He delivered one of the most famous speeches of all time, ***The Cross of Gold Speech***, where he advocated ***bimetallism*** (government use of both gold and silver), and the unlimited coinage of silver at a ratio of 16:1 with gold. At the end of the speech, he said that the Republicans were crucifying mankind upon a cross of gold. This meant that, if silver was not mixed with gold in the money supply, the farmer would financially die. Bryan passed away in 1925 shortly after defending creationism in the Scopes Trial (described later).

Definition: Election of 1896

Republican William McKinley defeated William Jennings Bryan (Democrat and Populist). It was an incredible mass media election, as Republican leader Mark Hanna spent nearly $4 million on McKinley's campaign. Money defeated the farmers yet again.

Definition: What exactly was the Progressive Era?

Answer: It was the period between c1890-c1918 that saw many reforms attempting to improve society. The movement looked to:

1. Make new rules for big business.

2. Give more rights to the people, and bring government closer to the people.

3. Clean up America after the Gilded Age.

Definition: Australian Ballot

It's a secret ballot. Before the Progressive Era, citizens declared their vote choices to their local election officials. This progressive reform looked to change that. The secret ballot was a Populist objective.

Definition: Sixteenth Amendment, 1913

This provided for a progressive or graduated

income tax that looked to end exploitation of the poor. It made wealthy people pay a greater share of taxes, or, "The more you make, the more they take." This was a Populist objective.

How to Remember: Tax has an X in it...so does SiXteenth

Definition: Seventeenth Amendment, 1913

This provided for direct election of Senators. Before this amendment, state legislatures appointed Senators. This change to the Constitution gave citizens a greater say as to who would represent them. This was also a Populist objective.

How to Remember: *Seeeeee*venteen... *Seeeeee*nators (it's the best we could do).

Definitions: Initiative, Referendum, Recall

These are ways to bring lawmaking to the people. These methods are still used today:

Initiative - Some states allow people to introduce bills to the state legislatures.

Referendum - Some states allow people to vote on certain bills.

Recall - Some states allow voters to remove incumbents (those originally elected) from office prematurely. In these cases, there would be a special election to find a replacement (or keep the incumbent).

Definition: Direct Primary

A direct primary is where the major political parties allow citizens to decide who will be nominated for the November Presidential and other local elections. Before primaries and nominating conventions, caucuses composed of men in "smoke-filled rooms" chose the candidates without consulting the people.

So now, for the path to the Presidency just remember that **P**encils **N**eed **E**rasers … **P**rimary + **N**ominating Convention + **E**lectoral College.

Question: What Progressive Presidents do I need to know?

Answer: Theodore Roosevelt - (1901-1909). McKinley was assassinated in 1901, and Vice President Roosevelt took over. He was a Republican, but acted more like a Democrat on certain economic issues. He battled trusts, was a friend to labor, and promoted conservation. One of the first people he invited to visit the White House was civil rights leader Booker T. Washington.

Woodrow Wilson - (1913-1921). A true Democrat, Wilson lowered tariffs, increased government control over the economy, and was President during World War I. He wasn't too big on civil rights though. He showed and marveled at D.W. Griffith's *Birth of a Nation* in the White House. The movie portrayed the KKK as heroes defending white women from the sexual advances of black men.

Also, do not underestimate the importance of Republican ***Robert La Follette***. Believed to be one of the greatest Senators of all time, the Wisconsin native was instrumental in passing much progressive legislation.

Question: Why was Theodore Roosevelt known as the *trustbuster*?

Answer: Roosevelt wanted to break up trusts that he saw as bad, yet keep the ones that did not exploit the consumer. Ultimately, the big companies busted in the Progressive Era were the Northern Securities Company (railroad), and John D. Rockefeller's Standard Oil.

Question: Was Teddy Roosevelt really a friend to labor?

Answer: He was in 1902 in the Anthracite Coal Strike.

In the Gilded Age, Presidents broke up strikes and supported employers. But Theodore Roosevelt sided with workers in this particular strike. He threatened to use force against the owners if they didn't agree to arbitration (fair negotiation with a third party).

Roosevelt said he gave those coal workers a **Square Deal**. His Square Deal platform meant that all middle class consumers should get a piece of the pie, instead of being dominated by big business.

Part of this platform included the Elkins Act of 1903 and the Hepburn Act of 1906. Both strengthened the Interstate Commerce Commission's ability to regulate unfair activities of the railroad industry.

Definition: *The Jungle*

Upton Sinclair hoped to reach Americans through their hearts, instead, he shocked them in their stomachs. *The Jungle* detailed the horrors of the meatpacking industry. Rat feces on meat, melted human flesh, and poisonous fertilizer in the sausage hoppers were just some of the putrid items featured in this work. Sinclair's book ultimately led to the **Meat Inspection Act, and the Pure Food and Drug Act of 1906** which created the Food and Drug Administration (FDA). Still around today, the FDA's job is to make sure that food and drugs are safe for human consumption. *The Jungle* made the meat industry safe for *both* workers and consumers.

Question: Besides Sinclair, what other muckrakers do I need to know?

Answer: Muckrakers looked to "rake up muck" (dirt) on society, and foster change through writing. Besides Sinclair, you should know about the following:

1. Jacob Riis - In 1890, he wrote *How The Other Half Lives*, a book detailing the impoverished immigrants who lived in overcrowded *tenement* dwellings of the Lower East side of New York City.

2. Ida B. Wells - c1893, she challenged Jim Crow, and promoted anti-lynching laws.

3. Ida Tarbell - *The History of the Standard Oil Company* was published in *McClure's Magazine* in 1904. It described the abuses of the oil monopoly. She received some credit for helping to break up that trust.

4. Helen Hunt Jackson - In 1881, she wrote *A Century of Dishonor*. As stated earlier, she challenged the United States Government's policy of imperialism against Native Americans.

5. Lincoln Steffens - His 1904 work, *The Shame of the Cities,* detailed corruption in municipalities, and hardships faced by immigrants.

Definition: Conservation

Theodore Roosevelt loved nature. He traveled to North Dakota as a young man to find himself. During his Presidency, he protected about 230,000,000 acres. Today, the National Park Service is indebted to him. Other big conservationists you should know are Gifford Pinchot and John Muir.

Definition: Election of 1908

Keeping with the two-term legacy of George Washington, Theodore Roosevelt went to Africa to hunt rather than seek re-election. He threw his weight (no pun intended) behind Republican William Howard Taft. Yes, Taft's the big guy who got stuck in the bathtub. Taft defeated William Jennings Bryan to take the White House.

Definition: Triangle Shirtwaist Fire, 1911

March 25, 1911 saw a horrific fire at a garment factory in New York City. 146 people were killed when locked doors prevented an escape. The exits were locked by employers trying to prevent employee work breaks. The fire led to stricter building and fire codes in cities across the country.

Definition: Ballinger-Pinchot Affair

Gifford Pinchot was the head of the US Forestry Division. He was a prominent conservationist, and a friend of Theodore Roosevelt. During the Taft Administration, Richard Ballinger was Secretary of the Interior, and he did not want to conserve. Pinchot attacked him in a letter, believing Ballinger had illegally helped others gain access to Alaskan coal fields. Pinchot was removed from office. The firing angered conservationists, and was an outrage to Roosevelt.

Definition: Election of 1912

Upset over Taft's policies, Roosevelt looked to violate the two-term tradition, and ran for President as the candidate of the *Progressive (Bull Moose) Party*. He was nearly assassinated during the campaign. Luckily an eyeglass case and long speech rolled up in his breast pocket swallowed the bullet.

Taft, a Republican, and Roosevelt, a former Republican, split votes. This made Democrat Woodrow Wilson the victor. Socialist Eugene V. Debs (former head of the American Railway Union) received 900,000 votes. He got about the same in 1920 when he ran from prison.

Definition: New Nationalism vs. New Freedom

The Election of 1912 saw two progressive candidates who wanted a more active role for the government in economic and social reform. However, they differed a bit in that:

Roosevelt's *The New Nationalism* would bust only bad trusts, while keeping the good ones.

Wilson's *The New Freedom* promised to bust more trusts than Roosevelt would. Wilson also wanted to lower tariffs.

Definition: Underwood Tariff, 1913

When Democrats are in office, tariffs (tax on imports) tend to go down as a benefit for consumers. The Underwood Tariff of 1913 brought tariffs to their lowest levels in many decades.

Remember for tariffs: **D** for **D**emocrats, **D** for **D**own. **R** for **R**epublicans, **R** for **R**aise.

Definition: Clayton Anti-Trust Act of 1914

Because the Sherman Anti-Trust Act of 1890 mostly busted unions, a redefinition of the act was in order. This new clarification gave more rights to unions, and opened the door to break up more monopolies/trusts. It also gave many new specific definitions as to what is "restraint of trade," including such things as price discrimination.

Definition: Federal Reserve Act, 1913

The Federal Reserve Act laid the foundation for our current central banking system, as the Federal Reserve System determines how the US dollar is circulated.

Definition: Federal Trade Commission, 1914

The FTC ordered corporations to refrain from unfair business practices such as false advertising. It also looked to stop potential monopolies. This protected consumers.

It must be noted that the Progressive Era increased the size of government *bureaucracies* (agencies with large numbers of workers). The FDA, FTC, Federal Reserve, and other new agencies made the government a much more complex web of offices. It would expand even further in the 1930s during the New Deal.

Definition: Eighteenth Amendment, 1919

The temperance movement of the early nineteenth century finally led to prohibition. Headed by women such as Annie Turner Wittenmyer of the *WCTU* (Women's Christian Temperance Union), prohibition meant that the sale and distribution of alcoholic beverages was illegal. Earlier, there were wet and dry states, as the sale of alcohol was a reserved (state) power. But this amendment changed everything. Note: The **21st** Amendment would repeal the **18th** in 1933. (**18** and **21** were also the last two drinking ages).

Question: What other female reformers of the Progressive Era should I know about?

Answer: Typically, women reformers of the Progressive Era were *middle class and educated*. Although the *Muller v. Oregon* decision (1908) said women should not work long hours, reformers were laboring hard at *settlement houses*. Settlement houses were places that gave shelter, meals, and advice to immigrants. You need to know:

1. Jane Addams - Addams helped establish Hull House in Chicago. Opened in 1889, this settlement house instructed English, and counseled immigrants on how to cope with America's big city life. Helping the poor was part of the Christian *Social Gospel* movement.

2. Florence Kelley - Similar to Addams, she was instrumental in New York City at the Henry Street Settlement.

3. Susan B. Anthony and Lucy Stone - Leaders of the women's suffrage movement (voting), they were members of NAWSA, the National American Woman Suffrage Association. Carrie Chapman Catt helped with suffrage at the grassroots level c1910.

4. Mother Jones - Labor reformer who spoke out against child labor, and for the wives of

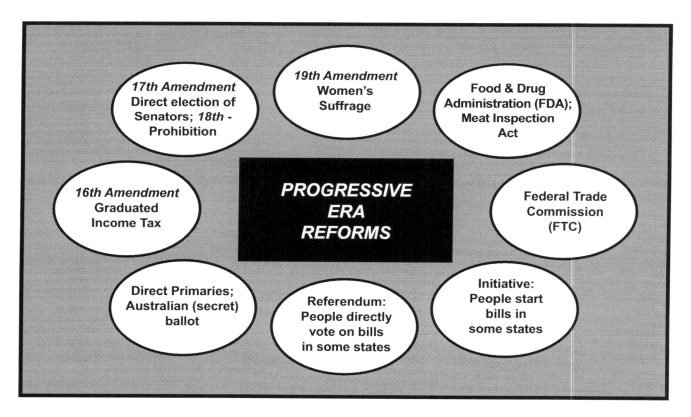

laborers. She was pro-union.

5. Pauline Newman and Emma Goldman - Union organizers. Strong women's unions of the time included the Women's Trade Union League and International Ladies' Garment Workers' Union.

Definition: Mothers' Pensions

A precursor to modern welfare assistance, these were state government cash payments to single-mothers. Not all states took part, but about 40 did so during the Progressive Era.

Definition: Nineteenth Amendment, 1920

Much like prohibition, women's voting rights were up to the states before 1919. In Wyoming, for example, women had full voting rights. In Nebraska, they could vote in Presidential Elections. In the South, they couldn't vote at all. This amendment gave women full voting rights in every state of the Union.

Question: What led to the end of the Progressive Era?

Answer: Some historians feel that the reform movement ran its course. But most likely it was the outbreak of World War I and the Red Scare (discussed later) which caused a backlash against the reformers, liberals, and socialists associated with the Progressive Era.

Review Questions

1. William Jennings Bryan's *Cross of Gold* speech called for
   A) the end of bimetallism
   B) the free and unlimited coinage of silver at a ratio of 16:1 with gold
   C) maintaining the gold standard, but printing more greenbacks
   D) exclusive use of soft money instead of hard money
   E) allowing only farmers to pay off their mortgages in specie

2. All of the following Populist ideas would become law in the Progressive Era EXCEPT:
   A) Direct Election of Senators
   B) Graduated Income Tax
   C) Unlimited coinage of silver
   D) Australian Ballot
   E) Railroad Regulation

3. A big supporter for creating anti-lynching laws in the early twentieth century was
   A) Jacob Riis
   B) Upton Sinclair
   C) Ida B. Wells
   D) Mother Jones
   E) Elizabeth Cady Stanton

4. *"This is no fairy story and no joke; the meat would be shoveled into carts, and the man who did the shoveling would not trouble to lift out a rat even when he saw one – there were things that went into the sausage in comparison with which a poisoned rat was a tidbit."*
   The above quote helped lead to which agency?
   A) Federal Trade Commission
   B) Food and Drug Administration
   C) Women's Christian Temperance Union
   D) Interstate Commerce Commission
   E) Federal Reserve

5. Jane Addams and Florence Kelley were best known for
   A) proclaiming a Declaration of Sentiments
   B) spreading the ideas of the Second Great Awakening
   C) muckraking to create social reform
   D) gaining universal suffrage
   E) aiding poor immigrants and helping them find jobs

6. Jacob Riis's journalistic work detailed
   A) unfair practices of cattle ranchers
   B) hardships of working in Southern factories
   C) terrible living conditions for new immigrants
   D) how alcohol consumption destroyed home-life
   E) civil rights abuses in the South after Reconstruction

7. Initiative, Referendum, and Recall were examples of

   A) ways to increase political participation in states
   B) reforms used for federal legislation
   C) Progressive reforms that were repealed before World War I
   D) limitations to the rights of workers
   E) programs that ended the spoils system

8. Theodore Roosevelt's Presidency

   A) lasted more than two terms
   B) took place during the years of World War I
   C) created the Underwood Tariff
   D) aimed to conserve national land
   E) passed federal anti-lynching laws

9. Why did Woodrow Wilson most likely secure the Election of 1912?

   A) His *New Freedom* was universally more popular than Theodore Roosevelt's *New Nationalism*
   B) The promise of the Underwood Tariff impressed Republican voters
   C) Theodore Roosevelt split the Republican vote with William H. Taft
   D) Wilson promised to trustbust less than his opponents
   E) William Taft's influence in the Ballinger-Pinchot scandal gave votes to Roosevelt

10. All of the following were passed or created in the Woodrow Wilson Administration EXCEPT:

   A) Underwood Tariff
   B) Clayton Anti-Trust Act
   C) Federal Reserve Act
   D) Federal Trade Commission
   E) Pure Food and Drug Act

Answers and Explanations

1. **B**. Bryan wanted to inflate prices so farmers could profit more from their crops to pay off their mortgages. Adding more silver to the currency would make money worth less, and inflate farm prices.

2. **C**. Bryan's ideas of bimetallism (gold and silver) never happened. To the Populists, that was the most important part of the Omaha Platform.

3. **C**. Ida B. Wells was outspoken for the creation of federal anti-lynching laws. A lynching was the murder, usually by hanging, of an African American. A lynching usually occurred in a mob, making prosecution difficult in the South.

4. **B**. This excerpt is from *The Jungle*. The book led to the Meat Inspection Act and the Pure Food and Drug Act (which created the Food and Drug Administration) in 1906.

5. **E**. Kelley and Addams set up settlement houses to help poor immigrants in cities.

6. **C**. Riis wrote *How the Other Half Lives* where he detailed the suffering of immigrants in urban areas.

7. **A**. Initiative and Referendum were reforms that allowed citizens in certain states to create bills, and vote on them. Recall allowed voters to take people out of office who were already serving their term (incumbents).

8. **D**. Roosevelt was a huge advocate for conserving federal land. Today, much of that protected land now belongs to the United States National Park Service.

9. **C**. Roosevelt was running as the candidate of the Bull-Moose (Progressive) Party, and Taft was the Republican candidate. Because Roosevelt was a former Republican, the two split the Republican vote. That left Wilson, a Democrat, the clear-cut winner.

10. **E**. The Pure Food and Drug Act of 1906 was passed during the Theodore Roosevelt Administration.

Imperialism and World War I, 1898-1919

The US was founded with a foreign policy based on neutrality, which was no longer feasible by 1898. The world was changing. Strong nations were taking over weaker ones for political and economic gain. The United States would act no differently. After acquiring territories in the Spanish American War, the US annexed Hawaii and incited a revolution in Panama to gain access to a canal. Along the way, they also angered the imperialized people of the Philippines and the government of Cuba. The US stayed neutral at the beginning of World War I. However, after the sinking of the *Lusitania*, issuance of the Zimmermann Telegram, and continual unrestricted submarine warfare by Germany, the US had no choice but to get involved in the war. After reading over the Treaty of Versailles, the Senate decided that America should return to a policy of isolationism. Consequently, the treaty was never ratified.

HERE IS WHAT YOU NEED TO KNOW:
Question: How did American foreign policy change c1898?

Answer: George Washington's policies of neutrality were no longer practical by 1898. The United States was looking to expand its growing empire, protect its trading interests, and secure territories around the globe. This meant the US would become *imperialists*, or a nation that looked to take over another country's resources and political life while imposing culture and trade upon them. The US needed markets for products, and sources of raw materials. This policy was an obvious break with both the principles of the Declaration of Independence and Washington's Proclamation of Neutrality.

Question: What were the causes of the Spanish-American War of 1898?

Answer: The two major causes were *The Boat and The Note*...but so were the following:

1. Jingoism - Ultra-nationalistic beliefs in the United States.

2. Support of Cuban uprisings for independence - The United States wanted Cuba to overthrow Spain and rid them from the Western Hemisphere. Violence had been occurring there for decades.

3. *Yellow Journalism* - This mostly stemmed from the competition between Joseph Pulitzer of the New York *World* and William Randolph Hearst of the New York *Journal*. "Yellow" came from the ink used in the newspapers. The term refers to the embellished stories of atrocities committed by the Spanish against the Cubans. The competing papers escalated claims that weren't always true.

The Boat - The USS *Maine*. We have since learned that this battleship sank on its own. Back then, it was blamed on a Spanish mine explosion.

The Note - The De Lôme Letter was written by a Spanish diplomat. The letter was greatly critical of President McKinley, calling him a weak leader. McKinley ultimately asked Congress to declare war.

Question: What were the results of the Spanish-American War of 1898?

Answer: Secretary of State *John Hay* called this, "a splendid little war" because:

1. The United States received Puerto Rico.

2. The US purchased the Philippines from Spain for $20 million. Note: You will need to know that US rule over the Philippines was quite harsh and led to massive resentment. The military had to put down a rebellion from 1899-

1902. This was the Philippine-American War.

3. The US received Guam.

4. Cuba became independent.

5. Not directly related to the war, but as the battle to secure the Philippines broke out, the US annexed Hawaii. This made businessmen like pineapple mogul Sanford Dole, very happy.

Definition: Insular Cases, c1905

Named for the Bureau of Insular Affairs, these were a group of Supreme Court decisions around 1905 that said the United States Constitution only partially applied to certain territories taken over during the Age of Imperialism. Alaska and Hawaii had full Constitutional rights. Places like the Philippines did not.

Definition: Teller/Platt Amendment

With Spain out of Cuba, the United States fluctuated with its foreign policy with the:

Teller Amendment - 1898 - The US said it would respect Cuba to govern itself.

Platt Amendment - 1901 - Just three years later, the US said it could look over Cuba's shoulder as it governed. The US could meddle in Cuban treaties and other domestic issues.

In 1903, the United States leased a 45 square mile area in Cuba known as Guantánamo Bay. It has since been used as a naval base.

Definition: Big Stick Diplomacy

Theodore Roosevelt said to "speak softly and carry a big stick." That meant to go about your business normally, but when the opportunity was right, or if something was for the taking, the United States would pounce on it.

Definition: Open Door Policy, 1899

1. The policy was negotiated by Secretary of State John Hay.

2. It said that China was open to all countries who wanted to trade. Of course, China had no say in this, as they were carved into zones controlled by foreigners known as *spheres of influence*.

Generally, the policy was created to protect American trading interests in China. They did not want to lose Chinese trade to other European countries.

Question: What do I need to know about the Panama Canal?

Answer: The canal connected the Atlantic and Pacific Oceans. Construction began in 1904. Here is how the US obtained the land:

1. Panama is an isthmus sticking out of Colombia…but back then it was controlled by Colombia.

2. Colombia did not want to honor the Hay-Herrán treaty that would have allowed the US to build a canal there.

3. John Hay told Panama if they wanted independence from Colombia, then America would back it.

4. After the successful Panamanian Revolution, the first order of business was approval of The Hay-Bunau-Varilla Treaty. This treaty granted the US the canal zone.

5. The building project was an immense one, with many dying from yellow fever.

Definition: Roosevelt Corollary to the Monroe Doctrine, 1904

This was a clarification to the 1823 Monroe Doctrine. The Monroe Doctrine was supposed to keep European nations from colonizing Latin America. However, when European nations reappeared in 1902 to collect debts, it angered the US. So, this corollary said that America would be the police power of the Western Hemisphere. Rather than have the Europeans in the Atlantic, the US would collect debts on their behalf.

Earlier in 1895, Secretary of State *Richard*

Olney told Britain that America was in charge of the Western Hemisphere. The British were looking to take land from Venezuela.

Definition: Dollar Diplomacy

Under President Taft, the US looked to invest abroad in China and Latin America.

Question: What caused the US to enter World War I in 1917?

Answer: Similar to the Spanish American War, it's good to know...*The Boat and The Note*

1. **The Boat** - The *Lusitania*. It was a passenger ship sailing off the coast of Ireland that was sunk by a German submarine (U-boat) on May 7, 1915. The US warned Germany to refrain from continued submarine warfare. However, the Germans would not stop.

2. **The Note** - *The Zimmermann Telegram*. In 1917, the British intercepted a telegram from German official Arthur Zimmermann. He was writing to Mexico seeking an alliance. He hoped for a Mexican invasion of America where territory lost in the Mexican War would ultimately be reclaimed.

The Germans continued their policy of unrestricted submarine warfare. President Woodrow Wilson asked Congress to declare war on Germany in April of 1917. He was hoping to make the world "safe for democracy."

Definition: National War Labor Board

It would be terrible if workers went on strike during a war. This Labor Board worked out differences between employers and employees during World War I. This was a good thing for unions who won better wages and shorter hours.

Definition: War Industries Board

This was a government agency that mobilized the domestic economy and oversaw the production of the supplies that were needed for the war effort.

Definition: Espionage (1917) and Sedition Act (1918)

Espionage Act - Threatened long prison sentences for disrupting the armed forces or the draft, which was created by the Selective Service Act of 1917.

Sedition Act - Targeted leftists/socialists who were against the war. The act made it illegal to speak out negatively against the government.

Definition: *Schenck v. United States*, 1919

Charles Schenck was a member of the Socialist Party. He distributed thousands of leaflets containing damaging language against the draft. He was arrested for violating the Espionage Act.

Weren't those leaflets free speech protected by the First Amendment? The Supreme Court said "no." Free speech was not absolute, as he was creating a "clear and present danger." According to Justice Oliver Wendell Holmes, Jr., Schenck's actions were like "shouting fire in a theater."

Question: Who took men's jobs during the war?

Answer: Since men (nicknamed doughboys abroad) were fighting in Europe, women and immigrants headed to the factories to fill the ranks. Also, African Americans · journeyed north for jobs in the *Great Migration* (discussed later).

Question: What happened with the Treaty of Versailles? Did the US ratify it?

Answer:

1. Democrat President Woodrow Wilson helped draft the Treaty of Versailles. A year earlier, he gave his famous *Fourteen Points* speech where he outlined his peace plans

85

for when the war ended. His fourteenth point was to have a permanent, international peace-keeping organization of nations, or a *League of Nations*.

2. The Senate must ratify treaties by a 2/3 vote, or they are not applicable to the United States.

3. The Republican-controlled Senate, led by Henry Cabot Lodge, had *reservations* regarding Article X of the covenant of the League of Nations. This was because it stated that nations in the League had to help other members who were threatened. The Republicans did not want to enter, as it would violate neutrality and perhaps bring European countries into the affairs of the Western Hemisphere.

Wilson collapsed and nearly died campaigning for the treaty. The US would never join the League, nor ratify the Treaty of Versailles.

Definition: Red Scare

After the Bolshevik (Russian) Revolution of 1917, there was a heightened fear of communism in America. Reports of bombings, and influxes of immigrants from Eastern European countries intensified this fear. *Attorney General A. Mitchell Palmer* ordered the arrest of anarchists, some labor leaders, and suspected socialists and communists. These arrests were done with little consideration for due process of law, as many were held for days without being charged with a crime. Collectively, they were known as *"Palmer Raids."*

Definition: Moral/Missionary Diplomacy

With regard to Latin America, President Wilson believed that the US had a moral obligation to only recognize democratic nations which were not oppressive or contrary to American interests.

Review Questions

1. All of the following contributed to the conflict leading up to the Spanish-American War EXCEPT:
   A) Sinking of the USS *Maine*
   B) Yellow journalism
   C) Sympathy for Cuba
   D) The De Lôme Letter
   E) President Taft's desire to continue Dollar Diplomacy

2. Theodore Roosevelt's Big Stick Diplomacy was most associated with actions in
   A) China
   B) Germany
   C) Panama
   D) Britain
   E) Japan

3. The United States supported the idea that they could control the Cuban government in the
   A) Teller Amendment
   B) Platt Amendment
   C) Roosevelt Corollary
   D) Zimmermann Telegram
   E) Olney Doctrine

4. The Hay-Herrán, and Hay-Bunau-Varilla Treaties were associated with
   A) the securing of the land for the Panama Canal
   B) keeping European nations out of the affairs of Western Hemisphere countries
   C) raising tariffs to keep imports from Latin America out of the United States
   D) bringing peace to the Spanish American War
   E) increasing tensions before World War I

5. The denial of Constitutional rights to some territories acquired in the late nineteenth century was affirmed in the
   A) Slaughterhouse Cases
   B) Teller Amendment
   C) Insular Cases
   D) Platt Amendment
   E) decision of *Worcester v. Georgia*

6. America struggled in an armed conflict to retain what imperialistic territory c1900?
   A) Puerto Rico
   B) The Philippines
   C) Guam
   D) Cuba
   E) Hawaii

7. The Zimmermann Telegram of 1917
   A) was sent by the United States Secretary of War to Britain asking for a firm alliance
   B) offered an end to unrestricted German submarine warfare
   C) was an attempt by Germany to form a Mexican-German alliance
   D) illustrated the need for America to remain neutral during the war
   E) announced the formal alliance between the United States and Russia

8. Which of a following was the main reason as to why Woodrow Wilson asked Congress to declare war in 1917?
   A) To protect American interests in the Caribbean
   B) Refusal of Germany to join the League of Nations
   C) The need to protect American interests in China
   D) Unrestricted use of German submarine warfare
   E) The sinking of the *Lusitania*

9. In the court case *Schenck v. US*, justice Oliver Wendell Holmes Jr.

A) defended rights of free speech

B) declared the Espionage Act unconstitutional

C) stated that free speech was not an absolute right

D) denied the right to suspend habeas corpus

E) affirmed unreasonable searches and seizures during a war

10. The US never ratified the Treaty of Versailles because

A) the treaty jeopardized American neutrality

B) the US did not want to meddle in Asian affairs

C) the financial cost of repairing Europe was too expensive for the United States

D) Henry Cabot Lodge's reservations were unconstitutional

E) the Treaty did not advocate for freedom of the high seas

Answers and Explanations

1. **E**. Dollar Diplomacy was a foreign policy of President Taft years after McKinley's War.

2. **C**. The "Big Stick" Policy was associated with countries in the Caribbean and Western Hemisphere, including Panama.

3. **B**. The Platt Amendment was the opposite of the Teller Amendment, as it stated that the US could control Cuban policy.

4. **A**. These were two of several treaties leading to the construction of the Panama Canal.

5. **C**. The Insular Cases were a series of Supreme Court decisions that limited Constitutional rights to certain new territories acquired during the Age of Imperialism.

6. **B**. The people of the Philippines took to arms in an attempt to gain independence. The US Army stood firm. After modernizing, the Philippines became independent in 1946.

7. **C**. German official Arthur Zimmermann sent the telegram to Mexico looking to gain an alliance. He promised a return of the American Southwest to Mexico after the war.

8. **D**. In the Zimmermann Telegram, Germany promised more unrestricted submarine warfare in the Atlantic. They delivered on this promise, bringing America into the war.

9. **C**. Holmes said that Schenck's distribution of anti-draft literature created a "clear and present danger," and would be like shouting "fire in a theater." Free speech was not absolute.

10. **A**. Under the leadership of Henry Cabot Lodge (the Lodge *reservations* to the treaty), the Senate would not ratify the treaty because it questioned America's neutrality. They did not want to join the League of Nations.

Roaring '20s Boom & Bust, 1920-1929

When people imagine the 1920s, they think *Boom and Bust*. The economy and social behaviors boomed throughout this decade. New changes to both male and female moral attitudes, coupled with excitement for consumerism and mass culture, signaled an end to traditional Victorian morals. However, all was not what it seemed. The KKK was growing in size, most farmers were still poor, and people worked long hours for little pay. A combination of overproduction, bank failures, bad credit, and shady stock market rules precipitated the Great Depression that lasted throughout the 1930s.

HERE IS WHAT YOU NEED TO KNOW:
Question: What was so roaring about the 1920s?

Answer: The stock market was booming, and new social identities were emerging. Some of the social roar included:

1. Mass culture excitement of movies, baseball, and amusement parks like Coney Island in New York.

2. People like Charles Lindbergh tested the limits of technology. In 1927, he received world-wide acclaim for flying solo from New York to Paris in 33½ hours.

3. A new woman emerged after World War I and the Nineteenth Amendment. (discussed later).

4. The automobile became a common mode of transportation. Henry Ford's *assembly line* mass produced automobiles like the Model T. Everyone on his assembly line did one task until the finished product was completed. The T was affordable to the middle class. It should be noted that the car affected the sexual revolution of the 20s, as women and men could now venture out alone. Previously, a chaperone would often go along.

Definition: The Lost Generation

Not everyone was thrilled in 1920. The Lost Generation was popularized by a group of writers who created literary characters that were disillusioned by materialism, and upset by the negative impact World War I had on them. Writers such as T.S. Elliot, Sinclair Lewis, and Ernest Hemingway were a part of this movement in literature.

Definition: Flapper

The New Woman of the 20s was armed with more than just the right to vote. Flappers mingled with men and challenged traditional Victorian values. Features of the flappers included:

1. Short dresses.
2. Makeup.
3. The "Bob" hair-style.
4. Smoking.
5. Mingling with men in public, and perhaps delving into the popular dance, *The Charleston*.
6. Sexual activity before marriage, as well as talking about once taboo subjects. *Margaret Sanger* began a campaign for birth control.

Definition: Great Migration

During and after World War I, many African Americans moved from the South to the North. Some came to fill the vacant jobs of the World War I soldiers fighting abroad. Others came with a desire to escape discrimination. Of course, discrimination would be ever-present in the North as well. American artist *Jacob Lawrence* detailed the migration in his paintings. This movement of millions of African Americans would continue throughout the twentieth century.

Definition: Marcus Garvey

Garvey was a proponent of black pride, separation, and African nationalism. He also sponsored a Back-to-Africa Movement which looked to bring African Americans to their land of ancestry. This movement was similar to the plans of the nineteenth century American Colonization Society.

Definition: Harlem Renaissance

Harlem, in upper Manhattan in New York City, was home to a flowering of African American culture on stage and in literature. The movement was highlighted by jazz music, like that of Louis Armstrong. Famous writers included Langston Hughes and Zora Neale Hurston.

Question: How successful was the Eighteenth Amendment at enforcing prohibition?

Answer: Not very. The 1919 *Volstead Act* was supposed to enforce prohibition. But people circumvented (went around) the prohibition amendment with:

1. Speakeasies - Places that secretly served alcohol when the cops weren't looking. Or, in some cities...the cops looked the other way after taking bribes.

2. Bathtub gin - Dangerous concoctions of alcohol that were made in people's homes.

3. Bootlegging - Illegal transportation and selling of booze. This type of behavior led to the rise of organized crime. It can be argued that Al Capone would not have been so powerful had it not been for the Eighteenth Amendment.

4. Some people just went to Canada for alcohol.

Definition: Scopes Trial, 1925

This was a controversial trial where Tennessee teacher John Scopes broke the law by teaching about Darwin's Theory of Evolution. In the trial, his lawyer, Clarence Darrow, cross-examined the prosecutor, former Presidential candidate William Jennings Bryan. Bryan claimed to be an expert on the Bible. Bryan won the case (popularly called "The Monkey Trial" at the time), but Darrow embarrassed him on the witness stand. The conviction was later overturned on a technicality. Bryan died shortly after the trial.

Definition: Sacco-Vanzetti Case

Ferdinando Sacco and Bartolomeo Vanzetti were two Italian-American anarchists who were convicted of murdering two men. The trial for murder was seen by many as unfair and containing faulty evidence. Nonetheless, the men were executed in 1927. Many viewed the case as an example of nativism (animosity towards foreigners).

Definition: Second Rise of the KKK

During World War I, *George Creel* headed the *Committee on Public Information* which provided propaganda that was pro-American. With an influx of immigrants coming over from Eastern Europe, there was a new movement in cultural nationalism called *100% Americanism*.

The Klan, which disbanded during Reconstruction, came back strong in the 1920s. Instead of only targeting African Americans, they now rallied against Jews, Catholics, and foreigners who didn't assimilate. By the mid-1920s, there were millions of Klansmen. Despite the violence, there were no signs of any federal anti-lynching legislation.

Definition: Teapot Dome Scandal

The biggest political scandal of the 1920s was the Teapot Dome Scandal during Warren G. Harding's Administration. In the controversy, public oil lands were sold to private speculators. Secretary of the Interior Albert Fall (hence the term "Fall Guy") was held accountable, and sent to prison.

Question: By the time it began in 1929, what were the causes of the Great Depression?

Answer:

1. Overproduction of crops. As seen in the Populist Era, farmers couldn't get high prices for their crops, so they produced more of them. This led to even *lower* farm prices.

2. Speculation (risky and excessive buying) of stocks. Because stocks could be purchased on margin (10% down with a promise to pay back 90%), they were being bought left and right. Stock prices boomed.

A name you should know is ***Andrew Mellon***. Mellon, Republican Secretary of the Treasury in the 20s, encouraged a bull market, promoted cutting taxes for the rich, and paid off some of the national debt. To remember him, just think: "If you were rich, wouldn't you eat a lot of Mellon?"

3. Buying on credit. Purchasing items on credit loans, similar to modern day layaway, became prevalent in the 1920s to help people buy all of the new products that consumerism had to offer. Refrigerators, irons, washing machines, vacuum cleaners...everyone wanted them, but not everyone had enough money to purchase immediately. Buying on credit was the solution, but not everyone could pay off their debts.

4. Bank failures. Banks don't hold all of your money. They loan it out or invest it. Panic led to bank runs, where people withdrew all of their cash before a failure could occur. This only accelerated bank failures. When banks failed, people lost their entire fortunes (no bank insurance existed until 1933). When people lost their money, they certainly couldn't pay back their stock margin or credit balances.

5. Stock market crash. All of the above led to stocks crashing on Black Thursday, and then again on Black Tuesday in October (24th and 29th) of 1929.

6. The depression that was already going on in Europe didn't help matters either, as foreign trade took a big hit by 1929.

Question: Did President Herbert Hoover do anything to help out during the Depression?

Answer: Yes he did, but only to some degree.

The common misconception is that he did nothing, and Franklin Delano Roosevelt did everything. Hoover did some work projects, like the Hoover (originally called Boulder) Dam. He also set up the ***Reconstruction Finance Corporation*** which provided about $2 billion to bail out states, banks, and corporations. But, Hoover was still blamed for the depression, as "Hoovervilles" (shantytowns) sprung up all over the country. His actions were considered "too little, too late," as many of them came months, or even years after the crash.

Hoover signed the ***Smoot-Hawley Tariff***. Though it was supposed to assist farmers competing with imported crops, by the time Hoover signed the law, it was the highest tariff since the 1828 Tariff of Abominations. It taxed imports so high that it decreased foreign trade, and isolated the American economy. Europe's inability to export to America further depressed the economy abroad.

Definition: Dust Bowl of the 1930s

Over-farming and Mother Nature combined to turn the soil to dust all over the western prairies. Parts of Kansas, Colorado, and especially Oklahoma were heavily hit, and many "Okies" moved to California. A famous photograph of a migrant farmer with her kids clinging to her was taken by Dorothea Lange during this long-term disaster. The Dust Bowl was famously portrayed in John Steinbeck's novel, *The Grapes of Wrath*.

Definition: Bonus Army

Thousands of World War I veterans assembled in Washington, DC and camped out in tents and huts in the summer of 1932. The veterans wanted to get their 1945 bonuses early, as the Depression made it difficult to find employment. Thus, they were hoping to lobby Congress to pass the Patman Bonus Bill. The Senate never passed it. After finally being told to disperse, the US Army, led by a young Douglas MacArthur, moved in with tear gas, and set fire to the veterans' tents and huts. The fiasco was a black eye for Hoover, and may have been a contributing factor in the loss of his re-election bid in the Election of 1932.

Review Questions

1. Republicans of the Gilded Age and 1920s supported
   A) low tariffs
   B) cheap railroad transportation for crops
   C) government regulation of industry
   D) unionization
   E) low taxes on the wealthy

2. Nativism (anti-foreign sentiment) could be seen in all of the following EXCEPT:
   A) The Molly Maguires
   B) Resurgence of the KKK
   C) Sacco-Vanzetti case
   D) Scopes Trial
   E) Emergency Quota Act

3. The "lost generation" in literature believed
   A) war was successful in galvanizing domestic nationalism
   B) the events of World War I gave many a sense of moral loss
   C) segregation was justified by laws of eugenics
   D) women should be allowed to pursue any career they wanted
   E) socialism was a feasible alternative to capitalism

4. How did flappers look to deviate from the Victorian norms of society c1920?
   A) They were able to secure equal pay
   B) After ratification of the Equal Rights Amendment, they were given equality under the law
   C) They dressed more provocatively, and pushed the envelope on moral behavior
   D) Unionization efforts were discouraged
   E) Women successfully campaigned for the repeal of prohibition

5. The chief proponent of the Back to Africa Movement was
   A) Marcus Garvey
   B) W.E.B. Du Bois
   C) Booker T. Washington
   D) Langston Hughes
   E) Zora Neale Hurston

6. The Harlem Renaissance can best be explained as
   A) a movement to end Jim Crow
   B) a celebration of African American culture
   C) a revival of industry in African American neighborhoods in the North
   D) an education movement in urban areas
   E) new beliefs in religion after Reconstruction ended

7. Which early 1930s event left Herbert Hoover at a disadvantage in the Election of 1932?
   A) Force used against the Bonus Army
   B) End of the Reconstruction Finance Corporation
   C) Support of the Hoover Dam project
   D) Bank failures after the creation of FDIC
   E) The Teapot-Dome Scandal

8. All of the following were causes of the Great Depression EXCEPT:
   A) Overproduction of crops by farmers hoping to gain a profit
   B) Failures of certain bank branches
   C) Buying products on credit
   D) Speculation of lands in specie
   E) Purchasing stocks on margin

9. Which of the following was a Great Depression program of Herbert Hoover?
   A) Security and Exchange Commission
   B) Reconstruction Finance Corporation
   C) Federal Deposit Insurance Corporation
   D) Agricultural Adjustment Act
   E) National Industrial Recovery Act

10. The novel, *The Grapes of Wrath*, by John Steinbeck is most associated with
   A) Smoot-Hawley Tariff
   B) The Dust Bowl
   C) The Bonus Army
   D) Coxey's Army
   E) The Great Migration

Answers and Explanations

1. **E**. Republicans of the 1920s supported big business, with tax cuts to the wealthy. Secretary of the Treasury Andrew Mellon helped the stock market roar through the 20s.

2. **D**. John Scopes was on trial for teaching about the theory of evolution. The "Mollies" were immigrants charged with kidnapping and murder. With sketchy evidence, 20 of the miners were executed in 1877. Sacco and Vanzetti were also immigrants executed with a lack of hard evidence. Furthermore, the 20s also saw a resurgence of the Klan, and quota acts to limit certain types of immigration.

3. **B**. A group of writers conveyed how a generation's optimism had been lost after the horrors of World War I.

4. **C**. A flapper was a woman who questioned traditional gender norms.

5. **A**. Marcus Garvey believed in Pan-Africanism, and a belief that African Americans should return to the homeland of their ancestors.

6. **B**. The Harlem Renaissance celebrated African American culture, and was centered in upper Manhattan.

7. **A**. The Bonus Army camped out in Washington, DC looking to get their World War I bonuses early. The US army, led by a young Douglas MacArthur, tear-gassed them. This was a very unpopular action during Hoover's Administration.

8. **D**. Specie, or gold and silver, was an issue during the Panic of 1837 in the days of Presidents Andrew Jackson and Martin Van Buren.

9. **B**. The Reconstruction Finance Corporation aimed to give financial aid to failing corporations and state governments.

10. **B**. Steinbeck's novel detailed the tragedy of the Dust Bowl and the destruction of farms and soil in the West and Midwest during the 1930s.

The New Deal of the 1930s

Herbert Hoover was blamed for the Great Depression. Voters wanted a more hands-on approach to the crisis, and elected Franklin Delano Roosevelt in 1932. Roosevelt promised a "New Deal" for America, and would be in office until his death during his fourth term in 1945. Roosevelt felt that it was the government's responsibility to help its citizens. The key focuses of the New Deal were creating jobs, reforming banks, limiting farm production, and regulating industry. However, not everyone agreed with Roosevelt's plans. Some, like the Supreme Court, thought he was overstepping his powers. Others, like Huey Long of Louisiana, didn't think the government was going far enough. The New Deal created an *alphabet soup* of programs that are a lot of fun to memorize.

HERE IS WHAT YOU NEED TO KNOW:
Definition: Election of 1932

Democrat Franklin Delano Roosevelt (FDR) defeated Republican Herbert Hoover in a landslide. Roosevelt campaigned with the promise of a "New Deal" for all Americans. The New Deal would differ from Hoover's approach, as Roosevelt planned to get the government involved in every aspect of the economy. His campaign song and slogan was "*Happy Days are Here Again*," which is what the organist played the night he was nominated.

Definition: RRR

Relief, Recovery, Reform...those were the three R's of the New Deal. Relief meant to provide a quick end to people's suffering. Recovery meant to get the economy back on its feet. Reform meant to pass legislation to make sure that a depression of that magnitude never happened again.

Definition: Fireside Chats

Roosevelt used the new media of radio to communicate the issues of the economy to all Americans. He called the citizens his "friends," and was a fatherly figure to many in a time of need.

Definition: John Maynard Keynes and Deficit Spending

Keynesian economics means deficit spending...to spend more money than you have. It was the theory of British economist John Maynard Keynes. The New Deal wanted to spend, spend, spend...so it could fix, fix, fix. This stimulation of the economy is called ***pump priming.*** By creating jobs, more people would have money to put into the economy. To increase revenue, the government can sell bonds and raise taxes.

Definition: The Hundred Days

Much of Roosevelt's sponsored legislation came in the first hundred days of his term. Roosevelt's "brain trust" of advisors helped him create his policies. The Hundred Days benchmark is still used today to evaluate Presidents during their first few months in office.

Question: How did Roosevelt look to fix the banking crisis?

Answer:

1. Two days after his inauguration, FDR called for a National Banking Holiday whereby all banks would be closed for four days as a cooling off period. The sound banks could then reopen with government permission.

2. The Emergency Banking Act of 1933 allowed the President to watch over banking transactions, and reopen solvent banks.

3. The Glass-Steagall Banking Act of 1933 created the *Federal Deposit Insurance Corporation* (FDIC) which insured all bank depositors up to $5,000.

Definition: SEC, 1934

The Security and Exchange Commission (still around today) was created to establish fair codes of stock trading. It also punished those who didn't play by the rules.

Definition: AAA, 1933

The Agricultural Adjustment Act was the solution to remedy the overproduction of crops of the 1920s. This act paid farmers to limit their crop productions. Yes, it paid farmers *not* to grow. The hope was that if the supply of farm products decreased, demand would increase, and so too would prices.

Question: How did Roosevelt look to fix the problem of unemployment?

Answer:

1. PWA, 1933 - The Public Works Administration, headed by Harold Ickes, looked to construct highways and buildings.

2. CCC, 1933 - The Civilian Conservation Corps paid about 3 million young men to dig ditches, improve natural landscapes, develop parks, and build roads.

3. TVA, 1933 - The Tennessee Valley Authority brought jobs and cheap power to the Southeastern regions near the Tennessee River. Much of the area did not have electricity at the time.

4. WPA, 1935 - The Works Progress Admin-

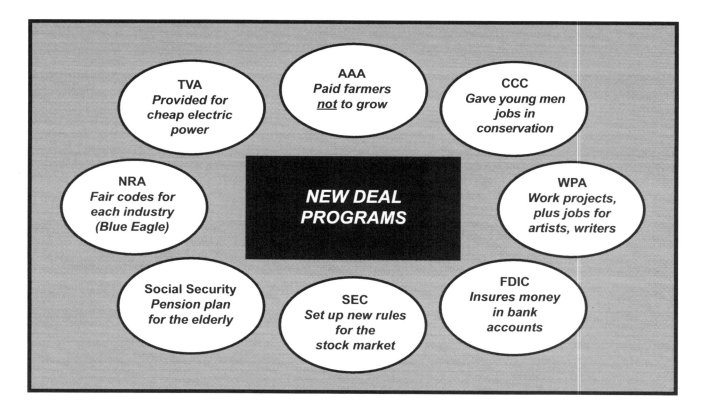

istration was created as part of the Second New Deal (explained later). It looked to employ artists and writers, as well as other laborers for building projects. Slave narratives (often inaccurate) were written to tell the stories of those former slaves still alive. Opponents of the WPA called it "boondoggling," or wasteful spending for jobs not needed.

Definition: NIRA and NRA, 1933

The National Industrial Recovery Act created the National Recovery Administration which allowed the President to set codes of fair practice (prices, materials, maximum working hours, etc.) for all industries. Businesses that successfully followed the codes were allowed to place a *blue eagle* in their window for all to see. The blue eagle became a symbol of patriotism.

Section 7a of the law gave collective bargaining to workers, and led to increased unionization.

Question: How did the Supreme Court tear apart the New Deal?

Answer: Congress and FDR supported the New Deal. The Supreme Court found parts of it unconstitutional. You should know these two cases:

1. *Schechter Poultry Corp. v. US* (1935) - The Supreme Court found that the President was in effect creating laws unconstitutionally, and NIRA was struck down. Congress creates laws, not the President.

2. *US v. Butler* (1936) - The Supreme Court found that the AAA was a violation of federalism (division of powers between the states and federal government). Like NIRA, AAA was destroyed by judicial review.

Definition: Court Packing Scheme

Since Justices are appointed for life, FDR tried to get around the Supreme Court any way he could. Congress has the right to increase the size of the Supreme Court. If they do so, the President, or FDR in this case, could then appoint liberal justices who supported his programs. His plan was to appoint six new justices to counterbalance existing justices over 70½ years of age. The packing scheme never happened, as it was quickly targeted by opponents to be a violation of power.

Definition: Second New Deal

The Second New Deal concentrated on "recovery and reform." Most important were:

1. WPA - Work Progress Administration (as discussed earlier).

2. Social Security Act, 1935 - Based on **Dr. Francis Townsend's** pension plan, this act, still around today, promised economic security for the elderly. However, because of the modern "graying" of the post-World War II Baby Boomer generation, today's Social Security has hit some financial obstacles.

3. Wagner Act, 1935 - reworded the NIRA to guarantee the right to unionize. This replaced Section 7a of the NIRA which was declared unconstitutional. It created the National Labor Relations Board (NLRB) to ensure that working rights were not violated. This led to an increase in the unionization of unskilled laborers. In 1935, **John L. Lewis**, the head of the United Mine Workers, formed the **Congress of Industrial Organizations (CIO)**, which rivaled the AFL until merging with them in 1955.

Question: What are some arguments that support the New Deal as a success?

Answer: Debating the New Deal could always be an essay. Here's how you can present the pro side:

1. The New Deal restored optimism.
2. It put an estimated 5 million people back

to work.

3. Although it expanded the federal government, it never broke away from democracy.

4. The government attempted to provide for the people rather than wait for the economy to take care of itself.

5. Some New Deal programs such as TVA, SEC, FDIC, and Social Security are still around today.

Question: What are some arguments that attack the New Deal as a failure?

Answer: ***Father Charles Coughlin*** used the radio in opposition of the New Deal. He wanted to nationalize the banks. ***Huey Long*** was a Democrat from Louisiana who thought the New Deal didn't go far enough. But to those who did not want to share wealth:

1. The New Deal made the government bureaucracy too big...even bigger than what came out of the Progressive Era.

2. There was still vast unemployment (World War II was what would get the US out of the Great Depression for good).

3. The government was exercising way too much power and bordering on dictatorship.

Review Questions

1. Among other things, the New Deal led to
   A) the creation of a national healthcare law
   B) adding a tenth member to the Supreme Court
   C) laws that forbid the unionization of workers
   D) some government control of industry
   E) the destruction of the welfare state

2. Which of the following is an example of a way in which Franklin Roosevelt raised the morale of the American people?
   A) Closing down all Hoovervilles
   B) Frequently addressing citizens through new media
   C) Attempting to appoint more justices to the Supreme Court
   D) Giving World War I veterans a stipend
   E) Allowing referendums on federal statutes

3. The Agricultural Adjustment Act of 1933 was New Deal legislation that looked to
   A) increase the amount of output in farms harvesting corn
   B) decrease the prices of overinflated farm goods
   C) give farmers a greater say in governmental politics in rural areas
   D) increase the size of livestock through selective breeding
   E) pay farmers not to harvest so prices could increase

4. All of the following were New Deal actions in the first Hundred Days of Franklin Roosevelt's Administration EXCEPT:
   A) Social Security Act
   B) Agricultural Adjustment Act
   C) Federal Deposit Insurance Corporation
   D) National Bank Holiday
   E) Civilian Conservation Corps

5. One major idea behind New Deal legislation was to
   A) provide for pure laissez-faire capitalism
   B) present opportunities for public works
   C) formally end the ability of the Federal Reserve to print money
   D) centralize power in the Judicial Branch
   E) decrease the scope of government control

6. The New Deal looked to fix unfair trading practices in the stock market with the creation of which of the following agencies?
   A) Securities and Exchange Commission
   B) Federal Deposit Insurance Corporation
   C) National Recovery Administration
   D) Federal Trade Commission
   E) Interstate Commerce Commission

7. The Supreme Court declared the National Industrial Recovery Act unconstitutional in the case
   A) *Miranda v. Arizona*
   B) *US v. Butler*
   C) *Schechter Poultry Corp. v. US*
   D) *Munn v. Illinois*
   E) *Muller v. Oregon*

8. Keynesian economics is best described as
A) printing money to cause inflation
B) spending more money than the government has
C) decreasing high paying jobs
D) insuring bank deposits
E) regulation of the stock market to ensure fair trading operations

9. Which of the following ideas from Dr. Francis Townsend was incorporated into New Deal legislation?
A) The Glass-Steagall Banking Act
B) The four day National Bank Holiday
C) The Blue Eagle
D) Social Security Act
E) Tennessee River Valley Authority

10. All of the following can be considered to be arguments against Franklin Delano Roosevelt's New Deal EXCEPT:
A) It would be manufacturing during World War II, not the New Deal, which ultimately saved the economy
B) The size of the government's bureaucracy increased to an even larger level than during the Progressive Era
C) Franklin Roosevelt's Executive Branch centralized too much power
D) The New Deal did not ultimately solve the nation's unemployment crisis
E) Franklin Roosevelt did not adhere to the principles of checks and balances

Answers and Explanations

1. **D**. The National Recovery Administration permitted the President to create fair codes of conduct for all businesses. This would later be declared unconstitutional.

2. **B**. The Fireside Chats were Roosevelt's radio communications with the public. He used the new media format of radio to try to calm the fears of the American people.

3. **E**. The AAA sought to limit crop production. The government wanted to reduce surplus so prices could rise.

4. **A**. The Social Security Act of 1935 came much later in Roosevelt's first term.

5. **B**. The crux of most of the New Deal legislation was paying people to work for government sponsored projects.

6. **A**. The SEC is still around today, and monitors the practices of the stock market.

7. **C**. The "sick chicken case" declared the NIRA unconstitutional, as the President was overstepping his powers by creating laws.

8. **B**. Deficit spending meant that the government should improve the economy by spending more money than it has. Think of the old adage, "it takes money to make money."

9. **D**. Townsend wanted a pension plan for the elderly. This idea influenced legislation for Social Security.

10. **E**. Roosevelt did listen to checks and balances. To FDR's dismay, when the Supreme Court declared acts unconstitutional, those laws were dead. The government then created new laws with different wording to appease the high court.

World War II, 1941-1945

Much like it did during the early years of World War I, the United States maintained neutrality at the beginning of Europe's Second Great War. However, soon after the Japanese attacked Pearl Harbor in 1941, the US was at war on two fronts...Europe and the Pacific. The same Americans who suffered in the Depression now had to save the world from fascism and aggression. After D-Day, the US and its allies were able to gain control of Europe. By island-hopping and dropping the atomic bomb, President Truman accepted an unconditional surrender from Japan. On the US Home Front, almost every citizen was able to contribute to the war effort. The Japanese on the west coast, however, were denied civil liberties and were forced to live in internment camps in unpopulated rural areas. The Supreme Court approved these measures.

HERE IS WHAT YOU NEED TO KNOW:
Question: What issues before 1941 should I know about?

Answer: In between the World Wars, the United States was neutral. At the *Washington Naval Conference* of 1921, major powers agreed to limit naval arms. The Kellogg-Briand Pact of 1928 renounced war as a form of national policy. In the 1932 Stimson Doctrine, the US refused to recognize aggressive Japanese takeovers in China. Here are some other things about the period just before World War II you should know:

1. Good Neighbor Policy - FDR improved relations with countries in Latin America because it was necessary to acquire allies in a dangerous pre-war world. Some wartime manufacturing took place in neighboring countries.

2. Neutrality Acts of 1935, 1937, and 1939 kept the US neutral, mostly in terms of arms shipments to foreign countries.

3. "Cash and Carry" was a 1939 policy proclaiming that the US would aid Britain. This was only if the British came to the US on their own ships, paid in cash, and then left with the weapons.

4. The Selective Service Act of 1940 was the *first ever peacetime draft* in American History.

5. The Destroyers for Bases Deal of 1940 avoided upsetting those who favored neutrality. FDR *traded* older large ships (destroyers) in exchange for British bases in the Caribbean. Giving or selling them would have been a breach of neutrality.

Definition: Lend-Lease Act of 1941

This act allowed the United States to sell unlimited weapons to the Allies. The buying was done on credit. Over $50 billion in supplies were sent overseas to allies (Britain, Soviet Union, France, and China).

Definition: Pearl Harbor, 1941

On December 7, 1941 the Japanese attacked Pearl Harbor, Hawaii by air. The sneak-attack resulted in 2,300 American soldiers killed, many of whom were aboard the USS *Arizona*.

After FDR's "Day of Infamy" speech, Congress declared war on Japan. Shortly after, Germany declared war on the US. The United States, Britain, France, and the Soviet Union were called the Allies. They fought the Axis Powers, which consisted of Germany, Italy, and Japan.

Question: What military events in Europe should I know about?

Answer:

1. The Allies began fighting in northern Africa and then went north to liberate Italy.

2. D-Day, June 6, 1944, was the largest battle and the turning point of the war. It led to the liberation of France. General Dwight D. Eisenhower was the Allied Commander.

3. The Battle of the Bulge during the winter of 1944-45 was the deadliest battle of the war for the Americans. However, Germany could not permanently break Allied lines.

4. Adolf Hitler of Germany killed himself on April 30, 1945 in an underground bunker. V-E (Victory in Europe) Day was proclaimed on May 8th after Germany surrendered.

Definition: Yalta Conference, 1945

The Yalta Conference gave the Soviet Union control over much of Eastern Europe. Though the Soviets promised free elections, these promises were empty, as nations were turned into satellites. It can be said that Yalta was the start of the Cold War.

At the conference, it was also agreed that the Soviets would enter the war against Japan, and Germany would be divided into zones of occupation. This Conference, held in the Soviet Union, occurred in the final days of FDR's life. When he died soon after, Vice President Harry Truman took over.

Other conferences to know about:

1. Tehran, 1943 - Here the Allies planned the end of the war strategy to defeat the Nazis.

2. Potsdam, 1945 - The Allies discussed the fate of Germany after they surrendered.

3. Nuremberg Trials - 22 Nazis were put on trial for the atrocities of the Holocaust. The trials began in 1945.

Question: What do I need to know about the War in the Pacific (Japan)?

Answer:

1. Douglas MacArthur was the commander.

2. The US followed a strategy of *island hopping* before reaching mainland Japan. Some of the islands attacked were Midway, Iwo Jima, and Okinawa.

3. Truman decided a mainland invasion of Japan would be too costly in terms of casualties, so he put in the order for the *Enola Gay* to drop *Little Boy* (the Atomic Bomb). On August 6, 1945 Hiroshima was bombed resulting in the deaths of about 140,000 people. Nagasaki was bombed three days later leading to an estimated 70,000 deaths.

4. Japan surrendered on August 15, 1945. V-J (Victory in Japan) Day would be on September 2nd.

Question: What are some arguments supporting the dropping of the atomic bomb?

Answer: The dropping of the atomic bomb could always appear on the essays. Here's how you present the pro side:

1. The bomb put a speedy end to the worst war in world history.

2. It showed the world, and especially the Soviets, that the US was a great superpower.

3. The Americans suffered terrible casualties in the Battle of Okinawa in 1945. A mainland invasion of Japan could have led to over one million casualties.

4. The Manhattan Project (bomb plan) cost about $2 billion. The bomb was a display of America's scientific investment.

5. The Japanese refused to unconditionally surrender. Adhering to the *bushido code*, *kamikaze* pilots would sooner die crashing into American ships than surrender.

6. The Japanese people were warned with leaflets describing the potential use of a new weapon. Still, there was no surrender.

Question: What are some arguments against dropping the atomic bomb?

Answer: Here's how you present the con side:

1. The Japanese were all but defeated. Even General Dwight Eisenhower believed the war could be won through conventional means.

2. Use of the weapon would lead to an arms race with the Soviet Union, and escalate the bitter Cold War.

3. The bomb was dropped on civilians. Hiroshima was not a military base, it was a city. The same could be said about Nagasaki.

4. Again, the Manhattan Project cost about $2 billion. Just out of the Great Depression, that was a lot of money to invest.

5. The environmental destruction was immense. No one knew for how long the water and soil would be poisoned.

6. The cancers and illness that would result from the bombing would be experienced by the people for decades to come. The dropping of the bomb was therefore immoral, and cruel and unusual punishment.

Question: What should I know about the American Home Front during World War II?

Answer:

1. Manufacturing boomed during the war. When the troops went overseas, women stepped into the factories. They were nicknamed *"Rosie the Riveter"* as the war progressed (a rivet is a bolt on a ship or plane).

2. Besides women, some Native Americans left their reservations to work in defense plants. They were also "code-talkers" in the war overseas. Communications in Navajo were never broken by the Japanese for the simple reason that no Native Americans lived in Japan.

3. Unions agreed not to strike so materials could continually be produced.

4. Rationing of meat, gasoline, and iron was critical to ensure that the troops had enough supplies overseas.

5. The war was paid for by a combination of increased income taxes and the sale of war bonds. Advertising campaigns would encourage Americans to purchase the bonds. The war cost about $288 billion, with just over 290,000 lives lost.

Question: What happened to Japanese Americans during World War II?

Answer:

1. Executive Order 9066 permitted the US Government to transform the west coast into a military zone.

2. About 120,000 Japanese Americans on the west coast were relocated and forced to live in *internment camps* spaced around the country. These citizens wound up losing their homes and wages. Most of the camps were in isolated areas. Remember, the President can suspend habeas corpus in a time of war.

Definition: *Korematsu v. United States*, 1944

Believing relocation was unconstitutional, Fred Korematsu refused to report to an internment camp. His criminal case went to the Supreme Court. The Court did not agree with him. The 1944 *Korematsu* decision stated that the Fourteenth Amendment, though guaranteeing equality in regular instances, could be denied in a time of war. Thus, Executive Order 9066 was constitutional. The federal government eventually acknowledged the regret of internment, and gave all survivors $20,000 in 1988. Korematsu's record was wiped clean.

Question: What were the domestic results of World War II?

Answer:

1. Soldiers returned and made babies. This was known as the Baby Boom.

2. The 22nd Amendment prevented another President from seeking a third term. FDR was elected to four terms because of the critical

situations at home and abroad.

3. World War II vets took advantage of the G.I. Bill (Servicemen's Readjustment Act), which offered free college, vocational training, and good loans on homes and business ventures.

4. After the War, there was a mass-exodus from the cities and a move to suburbia. President Dwight Eisenhower signed the *Federal-Aid Highway Act in 1956*. This provided for the modern day interstate highway system.

5. The 1950s saw a lot of *conformity* (9-5 jobs, and raising of families) in the suburbs. Such conformity upset people known as the Beatniks. The Beat Generation looked to experiment sexually or with drugs. They also rejected materialism, and sometimes practiced Eastern religions. The Beatnik book to know is Jack Kerouac's *On The Road*.

6. There was also a move to the *Sunbelt*, as cheap land was readily available in the South and Southwest.

7. Rosie the Riveter generally went back to the home, as women raised families in the conservative 1950s.

8. Going against conformity was *rock 'n' roll* music of the 1950s. Artists such as Elvis Presley combined African American blues, country, and jazz to create a new musical sound.

9. The *Taft-Hartley Act of 1947* hurt unions badly, as certain types of strikes were prohibited. Also, the act ended the *closed shop* (closed shops meant that one had to be in a union to work in a particular industry).

Question: What are the foreign policy results of World War II?

Answer:

1. The US and Soviet Union became superpowers, and the Cold War began.

2. Germany was divided into occupational zones controlled by the Soviet Union in the East, and Allies (Britain, France, and the United States) in the West.

3. The *United Nations* was formed as an international peacekeeping organization. The US, Soviet Union, France, Britain, and China would be the Five Permanent Nations with veto power. The UN grew out of the *Atlantic Charter* of 1941, where Winston Churchill of Britain, and FDR agreed to stabilize the world with peace when the war ended. Unlike the League of Nations, the UN can assemble peacekeeping troops. Also, unlike the League, the US joined the UN.

Review Questions

1. The Lend-Lease Act
   A) allowed America to continue its policy of imperialism in China
   B) provided $50 billion worth of supplies to Allied Nations during World War II
   C) kept foreign nations from colonizing in the Western Hemisphere
   D) affirmed America's neutrality during the First World War
   E) lent bases to Britain in exchange for bases in the Caribbean

2. American citizens helped out the effort of World War II by doing all of the following EXCEPT:
   A) Purchasing war bonds
   B) Donating scrap metal
   C) Rationing meat
   D) Paying more income taxes
   E) Striking to ensure workers' rights in defense plants

3. The United States ended their policies of neutrality in the 1940s when
   A) the Japanese attacked Pearl Harbor
   B) Germany continued a policy of unrestricted submarine warfare
   C) Italy declared war on the United States
   D) Germany threatened to align with Mexico
   E) United States boats were sunk in the Atlantic

4. Which of the following was the main reason why Harry Truman ordered the dropping of the atomic bomb?
   A) Dropping the bomb would lead to an arms race with the Soviet Union
   B) He wanted to end the war in Europe
   C) If the bomb was successful, it would prevent a mainland invasion of Japan
   D) The military base it was dropped on was equipping more than half of the Japanese arsenal
   E) To make the invasion of Tokyo feasible, the surrounding islands had to be bombed

5. During the war, Japanese Americans on the west coast
   A) filled the ranks of integrated regiments
   B) were relocated to internment camps
   C) were denied freedom of speech
   D) refused to pay their taxes
   E) were the main buyers and sellers of war bonds

6. In *Korematsu v. US,* the Supreme Court ruled that
   A) the Fourteenth Amendment was absolute
   B) the Japanese were permitted to own property within internment camps
   C) in times of war, Constitutional rights could be limited
   D) habeas corpus rights were universally guaranteed
   E) curfews for Japanese Americans were not constitutional

7. The turning point of the war in Europe occurred in the
   A) invasion of northern France at Normandy
   B) Battle of the Bulge
   C) invasion at Pearl Harbor
   D) Battle of Iwo Jima
   E) invasion of Belgium

8. The Yalta Conference presented which potential conflict?
   A) A struggle for land between Britain and the United States
   B) The spread of communism throughout Eastern Europe
   C) The unification of Germany
   D) A nuclear arms race between Western nations
   E) The exchanging of political prisoners

9. The two superpowers that came out of World War II were
   A) Britain and the United States
   B) Soviet Union and the United States
   C) Britain and France
   D) Soviet Union and Britain
   E) Soviet Union and France

10. The GI Bill
   A) created a peacetime draft
   B) promised college tuition and loans to soldiers returning from World War II
   C) hoped to discourage settlement in the Sunbelt after World War II
   D) led to a gradual reduction of troops in Western Europe
   E) created municipal public works projects in the west for veterans

Answers and Explanations

1. **B**. In 1941, the United States aided Britain, and later other allies, with an immense loan of supplies.

2. **E**. Unions were encouraged not to strike. Strikes would disrupt supply lines for the war effort.

3. **A**. The attack on Pearl Harbor drew the United States into the war.

4. **C**. Truman believed a mainland invasion of Japan would be too costly in terms of American troop casualties.

5. **B**. Because a small number were perceived to be a potential threat, all Japanese Americans in western "military zones" were relocated to internment camps. These camps were generally in unpopulated rural areas.

6. **C**. The Supreme Court ruled that Executive Order 9066 was constitutional. Therefore, during the war, Japanese people could be relocated.

7. **A**. The turning point was D-Day, the invasion of Normandy in Northern France.

8. **B**. When Soviet leader Joseph Stalin gained control of the former Nazi-controlled lands, they became communist satellites of the Soviet Union.

9. **B**. The United States and Soviet Union would be engaged in the Cold War as superpowers from 1945-1991.

10. **B**. The GI Bill offered tuition, vocational training, and home loans to World War II veterans returning from battle.

The Cold War, Korea/Vietnam 1945-1991

After World War II, the United States and Soviet Union remained the only superpowers in the world. Although the two countries never directly fought, they antagonized each other throughout the Cold War. A space race, blockade of Berlin, spy plane controversy, and near nuclear war over Cuba, were just some of the issues during these tense decades. The two fought "puppet wars," as America's policy to contain communism led to conflicts in both Korea and Vietnam. The War in Vietnam proved to be incredibly unpopular among the young generation of Americans, and led to a harsh backlash against the government.

HERE IS WHAT YOU NEED TO KNOW:
Question: Why was it called a Cold War?

Answer: No, it's not because it's cold in Russia. The Cold War was fought (or not fought) between the US and the Soviet Union from 1945-1991. Although they never directly attacked one another, there were puppet wars at times, like Korea and Vietnam. One could argue that it's called a Cold War because bullets are hot and none were fired at each other. You might also say that the US and Soviet Union displayed cold feelings towards one another. Whatever the reason, Americans lived in fear of a nuclear war for many years.

Question: What were the differences between the US and USSR?

Answer: United States: Political system is democracy, and economic system is capitalism.

Soviet Union: Political system was dictatorship, and economic system was socialism. Dictatorship + Socialism = Communism, and complete government control.

The US wanted to: 1) contain communism, 2) rebuild Eastern Europe to provide the US with new markets for products, and 3) reunite Germany.

The Soviet Union wanted to: 1) spread communism, 2) control Eastern Europe to protect Soviet borders, and 3) keep Germany divided.

Definition: Containment

US diplomat George Kennan coined this term that meant preventing the spread of communism. This was typically done by forming alliances with weaker countries to fend off communist aggression. Containment is the opposite of appeasement (giving in to what the aggressor wants). Containment is also the most important term of the Cold War. Why did we go to Korea? Containment. Why did we go to Vietnam? Containment. Why did we spend so much money on the military? Containment. Below is a foreign policy time-line for American History.

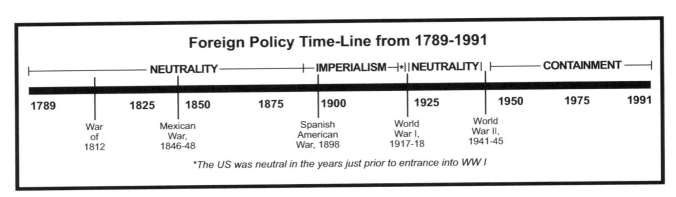

Foreign Policy Time-Line from 1789-1991

	NEUTRALITY			IMPERIALISM	*NEUTRALITY		CONTAINMENT	
1789	1825	1850	1875	1900	1925	1950	1975	1991
	War of 1812	Mexican War, 1846-48		Spanish American War, 1898	World War I, 1917-18	World War II, 1941-45		

The US was neutral in the years just prior to entrance into WW I

Definition: Truman Doctrine, 1947

The doctrine gave military aid (no troops) to countries resisting communism. Greece and Turkey took advantage of the aid.

Definition: Marshall Plan, 1947

This was Secretary of State George Marshall's strategy to give economic aid to countries that were not communist. The idea was to make countries stronger and less susceptible to communist takeovers. About $12.5 billion was given to nations all over Europe.

Definition: Berlin Airlift, 1948

Soviet leader Joseph Stalin, wanting to keep Germany divided, blockaded highways and railroads going into West Berlin (the non-communist side). He hoped this would make West Berlin dependent upon him and his satellites for supplies. However, the US and Britain sent 277,000 flights loaded with food and necessities for the German people. A furious Stalin thought the airlift might lead to war with the US. But, as with everything else in the Cold War, direct conflict was avoided.

Definition: NATO vs. Warsaw Pact

Think of these two as the gangs of the Cold War. NATO (North Atlantic Treaty Organization) was founded in 1949 and supported democracy. The Warsaw Pact, consisting of the Soviet Union and their satellites, was founded in 1955 and was referred to more commonly as the Communist Bloc.

Definition: Senator Joseph McCarthy and Communist witch-hunts

McCarthy was a Republican Senator from Wisconsin in the 1950s. *McCarthyism* was a witch-hunt that looked to sniff out communists both in government and general American society. It was similar to the Red Scare of A. Mitchell Palmer after World War I. Many Hollywood entertainment figures were targets.

In addition to McCarthy, there was HUAC (The House Un-American Activities Committee) which also looked to arrest suspected communists. The most famous government official targeted by HUAC was Alger Hiss. He was found guilty of perjury after he denied being a communist spy.

The government was watching average citizens as well. In the 1951 case of *Dennis v. US*, the Supreme Court ruled that speech advocating for an overthrow of the government was not protected by the First Amendment. Eugene Dennis of the American Communist Party had violated the Smith Act of 1940, which made such talk a crime.

Definition: Julius and Ethel Rosenberg

Accused of selling nuclear secrets to the Soviets, the Rosenbergs' 1951 court case kept the country on edge. They pled the Fifth Amendment (remained silent), and were convicted. They were later executed in 1953, becoming the first civilians ever to be put to death for treason.

Definition: Sputnik, 1957

In 1957, the Soviets successfully launched a satellite named Sputnik into space. Not only did this make Americans nervous about Soviet technology, but it gave the US a feeling of inferiority. The result of Sputnik's launch was an increase in spending on American education and science. In 1969, the US would win the space race to the moon.

Definition: U-2, 1960

It's not the rock band. But, if you look at some of their cover art, you will see a plane. The U-2 was a spy plane that was shot out of the Soviet sky in 1960. Although the US denied

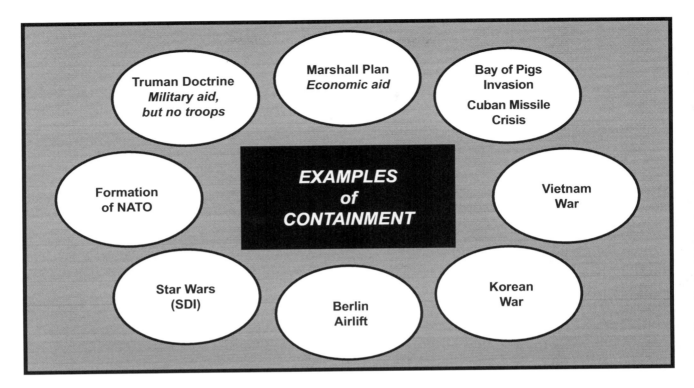

EXAMPLES of CONTAINMENT

- Truman Doctrine
  Military aid, but no troops
- Marshall Plan
  Economic aid
- Bay of Pigs Invasion
  Cuban Missile Crisis
- Formation of NATO
- Vietnam War
- Star Wars (SDI)
- Berlin Airlift
- Korean War

a spy plane was flying behind the iron curtain (metaphor for the Communist Bloc's border), the evidence was clear. Francis Gary Powers, the pilot, was held captive. The incident proved that distrust between the superpowers was real, and other spies were likely attempting to infiltrate both borders.

Definition: H-Bomb

The H-Bomb, or Hydrogen Bomb, worked on fusion. It was 1,000 times more powerful than the Atomic Bomb that worked on fission. The fear of a nuclear war was the underlying story of the Cold War, as it led to "duck and cover" drills, as well as the creation of bomb shelters.

Definition: Brinkmanship

This meant going to the brink of war, but coming just short of fighting. The escalation of brinkmanship peaked from 1961-1962 under President John F. Kennedy.

Definition: The New Frontier

John Fitzgerald Kennedy would only be President for a few years, but they would be important ones in the Cold War. His Presidential Election of 1960 promised a New Frontier. Kennedy supported civil rights and helping the poor. He started the Peace Corps, and led America during the tense Cold War years of the early 1960s.

Definition: Berlin Wall

In 1961, Nikita Khrushchev's Soviet Union built a wall that would formally divide communist East Berlin from non-communist West Berlin. Kennedy traveled to the wall to deliver his famous *Ich Bin Ein Berliner* (I am a Berliner) speech. He told the people of Berlin that the rest of the world was behind them. It is disputed that what Kennedy said translated to "I am a doughnut" in the speech (a Berliner is also a jelly doughnut). In 1987 President Ronald Reagan traveled to Berlin to give his famous, "tear down this wall" speech as a challenge to Soviet leader Mikhail Gorbachev. The wall came down in 1989.

Definition: Bay of Pigs Invasion, April 17, 1961

Fidel Castro, a communist, took over Cuba in 1959. Having a communist country just 90 miles from the United States was a scary thought to most Americans. Kennedy wanted to get rid of any nearby communist influence. The US supported a rebellion led by Cuban exiles. They were defeated at the Bay of Pigs in Cuba. Not only did the US sponsor the failed rebellion, but the event strengthened the legitimacy of Castro.

Remember: The US helped free Cuba from the Spanish back in 1898. But, the Platt Amendment of 1901 said that the US could meddle in Cuban affairs. Bad relations caught up with the US by the 1960s.

Definition: Cuban Missile Crisis, October of 1962

The closest the United States and Soviet Union ever came to nuclear war was during these two weeks of October. After the Bay of Pigs Invasion, Cuban and Soviet relations were quite good. So good, in fact, that the Soviets moved missiles into Cuba that could be used to destroy American cities. When US intelligence learned of this, Kennedy took it as a threat of war. His solution was to:

1. Blockade (quarantine) Cuba by surrounding it with US naval ships to prevent the delivery of additional Soviet weapons.
2. Threaten force if Khrushchev did not remove the missiles.

Cooler heads prevailed, and Khrushchev removed the missiles. In return, the US agreed not to invade Cuba. Furthermore, the US removed missiles of their own from Turkey.

Definition: Détente

This means an easing of Cold War tensions. The Cuban Missile Crisis scared the heck out of everyone. The 1970s saw friendlier diplomacy between the two superpowers. President Richard Nixon and Soviet leader Leonid Brezhnev were sometimes seen smiling together. The key détente event to know is:

SALT - Strategic Arms Limitation Talks. This was a treaty in 1972 that limited the number of nuclear weapons each country had in their arsenal. Of course, this was all a charade, as no one knew for sure how many weapons each country had stockpiled.

Definition: Star Wars/Strategic Defense Initiative

President Ronald Reagan abandoned détente. His Strategic Defense Initiative was an elaborate technological endeavor that looked to zap missiles out of the sky. The plan sounded like science fiction, so it was nicknamed *Star Wars*. The Soviet Union began to collapse internally during Reagan's Presidency, and the Cold War was over by 1991.

KOREA AND VIETNAM
Question: What do I need to know about the Korean War?

Answer:

1. Because Truman had integrated the army in 1948, African Americans and whites fought *side-by-side* for the first time in Korea (blacks had been in separate regiments since the Civil War, most notable were the distinguished ***Tuskegee Airmen*** pilots of Word War II).

Note that Truman's stance on Civil Rights affected the Presidential Election of 1948. Southern Democrats abandoned their party and formed the segregationist States' Rights Democratic Party, or ***Dixiecrat Party***, and ran Strom Thurmond of SC for President. Truman

114

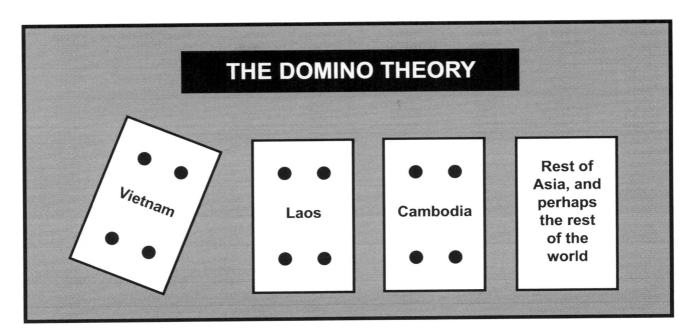

THE DOMINO THEORY

Vietnam

Laos

Cambodia

Rest of Asia, and perhaps the rest of the world

still won the election. As President, he promised a *Fair Deal*, which meant social improvement, civil rights, and expanding education and healthcare. Remember: "Tru" was "Fair."

2. Korea was an undeclared war. The UN voted to send in troops after communist North Korea crossed the 38th parallel and attacked non-communist South Korea in 1950.

3. Harry Truman fired Douglas MacArthur from command. MacArthur challenged Truman's decisions publicly. Truman, as Commander-in-Chief, fired him.

4. The war ended in 1953 during Dwight Eisenhower's Administration. Massive American aid poured into South Korea for decades. The 38th parallel is still the dividing line today. 33,746 Americans were killed in Korea.

Definition: Domino Theory

First appearing during the Eisenhower Administration, this was the belief that if one nation in Asia fell to communism, the rest of the nations would also fall...like dominos. It was important to stop that first country from becoming communist. See Domino Theory illustration above.

Definition: Eisenhower Doctrine

This allowed foreign countries to request economic or military aid if they were being threatened by another nation (specifically, it was aimed at Soviet interests in the Middle East).

Definition: Military-Industrial Complex

When Eisenhower left office, he warned of the military-industrial complex. The term refers to the money-relationships between legislators, the Pentagon (military), and industry. This web of money, weapons, and the people who make foreign policy could lead to corruption.

Definition: Gulf of Tonkin Resolution

In 1954, the French saw their Vietnamese city of Dien Bien Phu fall to the communists, and their leader Ho Chi Minh. Under Eisenhower and Kennedy, there was a gradual escalation of a US military presence in Southern Vietnam. When JFK was assassinated in 1963, Vice President Lyndon B. Johnson became President.

In 1964, at the Gulf of Tonkin in Vietnam,

American ships were fired on (the severity of this was likely embellished). After the event, Congress approved the Resolution which gave Johnson a "blank check" to use the military as he saw fit in Vietnam. This meant a large escalation of American forces.

Definition: Vietcong

The Vietcong were communist guerilla soldiers in *South* Vietnam. Vietnam was divided at the 17th parallel. As with Korea, the communists were supposed to be in the North... not the South.

Question: Militarily, what do I need to know about the Vietnam War?

Answer:

1. Much of the war was fought on dangerous terrain in a jungle.

2. Napalm was an explosive chemical that was used extensively in Vietnam. Agent Orange was a chemical used to remove leaves from the trees where guerilla soldiers were positioned. Years later, this chemical was known to cause cancer in many Vietnam veterans.

3. The Tet (lunar New Year) Offensive of 1968 was a massive thrust southward by the communists in the North. Although the United States pushed back the attack, it had a catastrophic affect on American morale, while increasing support for the communists within Vietnam.

4. In 1973, President Richard Nixon ended US involvement with the ***Paris Peace Accords.*** Vietnam became communist shortly thereafter.

Question: What do I need to know about the anti-war movement?

Answer:

1. In the 1950s, there were Beatniks (who experimented with drugs and sex while condemning war and materialism) such as Jack Kerouac, who wrote the book, *On the Road*. By the 1960s, the Beatnik movement had inspired ***hippies*** who protested the war and the military draft.

2. Folk musicians such as Bob Dylan sang for peace. Others sang against the military draft that affected thousands of young males. Phil Ochs sang against the draft in his song *Draft Dodger Rag*. Other folk musicians to know were Pete Seeger and Tom Paxton. Arlo Guthrie famously protested the draft with his song *Alice's Restaurant*. The negative energy surrounding Johnson led him to abandon plans to seek a second full term in 1968.

3. At Kent State University in 1970, a war protest turned violent when the Ohio National Guard fired on students, killing four. Most protesters against the war were young. Young men were impacted the most, as they were subject to the draft. In 1971, the Twenty-sixth Amendment lowered the voting age to 18, thus giving the younger generation a say in government. It was said that men were old enough to fight in Vietnam, but not old enough to vote.

Definition: Vietnamization

Richard Nixon's plan to *gradually remove US troops* from Vietnam was called Vietnamization. He hoped to turn the war over to Vietnamese soldiers. The US pulled out for good in 1973. There were 47,355 combat deaths during the duration of the war, plus many POW-MIA (Prisoners of War, Missing in Action).

Definition: Nixon Doctrine, 1969

Nixon's policy stated that the United States would not provide extensive manpower in future Asian wars, but would still give military and economic aid when aggressors threatened nations in need. The US, however, would still carry out their current treaty agreements.

Review Questions

1. George Kennan's view of the policy of containment meant
   A) appeasement to the Soviet Union
   B) an attack on the Soviet Union and its satellites
   C) the division of Germany into zones controlled by the West and Soviet Union
   D) stopping both the spread of communism and Soviet Union interests
   E) a decrease in tensions and more diplomacy

2. The Truman Doctrine
   A) offered combat troops to help countries fighting communism
   B) gave economic aid to scientists developing the H-Bomb
   C) provided military aid, but not troops, to foreign countries threatened by communism
   D) looked to expand democracy to areas in the Middle East
   E) was repealed by Congress in favor of the Marshall Plan

3. How did American foreign policy post-World War I compare to policy post-World War II?
   A) After World War II, the United States returned to an isolationist foreign policy
   B) The lessons of joining the League of Nations prevented alliances in a post World War II world
   C) The Senate never approved admission into the United Nations
   D) After World War I, the United States practiced a greater degree of brinkmanship
   E) The United States agreed to join an international peace-keeping organization after World War II

4. All of the following were associated with the Cold War EXCEPT:
   A) Bay of Pigs Invasion
   B) Strategic Defense Initiative
   C) U2 Incident
   D) SALT
   E) National Origins Act

5. McCarthyism of the 1950s was most similar to
   A) Japanese internment during World War II
   B) suspension of habeas corpus in the Civil War
   C) the immigration quota laws of the 1920s
   D) Palmer Raids of the World War I Era
   E) Jim Crow laws in the American South after Home Rule

6. What was John F. Kennedy's main course of action during the Cuban Missile Crisis?
   A) A threat of force and a strict quarantine of Cuba
   B) A calculated invasion of the Cuban mainland at the Bay of Pigs
   C) Diplomacy with Nikita Khrushchev which led to the disarmament of missiles in exchange for American bases in the Caribbean
   D) A treaty with the Cubans which transferred the missiles to Poland
   E) Cuban prisoners of war were exchanged for disarmament of the missiles

7. Détente is most associated with
   A) The Marshall Plan
   B) The Truman Doctrine
   C) Strategic Arms Limitation Talks
   D) The Vietnam War
   E) Berlin Airlift

8. Why was the Tet Offensive significant?

A) It led to a takeover of South Vietnam by the Vietcong

B) When the Northern Vietnamese moved south, it decreased the morale of American forces

C) It was the deciding battle in the American victory over the communists in Vietnam

D) Ho Chi Minh's proclamation of victory led to American withdrawal of troops

E) Johnson received Congressional approval to escalate the War in Vietnam

9. The Gulf of Tonkin Resolution

A) led to the policy of Vietnamization

B) allowed President Nixon to pull out of Vietnam

C) led to the escalation of the War in Vietnam

D) denied due process of law to Vietcong prisoners

E) outlawed the use of napalm in rural villages

10. How did Richard Nixon's Doctrine compare to the Domino Theory of Dwight Eisenhower?

A) Nixon promised to use nuclear force if necessary

B) Eisenhower hoped to stop the spread of communism in Europe, whereas Nixon was concerned with Southeast Asia

C) Eisenhower would only aid foreign nations when they were being threatened by a nuclear power

D) Nixon would no longer commit to extensive ground troops in Asian Wars

E) Nixon refused economic aid to any country

Answers and Explanations

1. **D**. Containment meant to stop the spread of communism. That was the main objective of all Cold War policies. Kennan's name is associated with containment.

2. **C**. Greece and Turkey took advantage of the Truman Doctrine's military aid.

3. **E**. The United States joined the United Nations after World War II. After World War I, the US did not join the League of Nations.

4. **E**. The National Origins Act limited immigration from Eastern Europe during the 1920s.

5. **D**. The Bolshevik (Russian) Revolution of 1917 caused a Red Scare in the United States. Palmer, the Attorney General, went on a witch-hunt similar to McCarthy's.

6. **A**. Kennedy threatened an invasion of Cuba after a strict quarantine. Khrushchev removed the missiles from Cuba, and the United States disarmed some of theirs in Turkey.

7. **C**. Détente meant a lessening of Cold War tensions. SALT was a treaty that limited nuclear missiles in both the United States and Soviet Union.

8. **B**. The Tet Offensive was when the North Vietnamese pushed South. This led to a decrease in American morale.

9. **C**. The Gulf of Tonkin Resolution gave President Johnson a "blank check" for dealing with the military crisis in Vietnam.

10. **D**. The Nixon Doctrine looked to limit the use of American troops in Asian conflicts.

Civil Rights

Jim Crow, or segregation laws, had been in effect for a century. In 1954, things changed when the Supreme Court unanimously declared "separate but equal" in schools to be unconstitutional in the *Brown v. Board of Education* decision. The goals of civil rights leaders differed. Some, like Martin Luther King Jr., wanted a harmonious blending of the races in society. Others, like Malcolm X, called for black separation. Despite the Civil Rights Act of 1964 which declared discrimination illegal, there was still work to be done by civil rights leaders.

HERE IS WHAT YOU NEED TO KNOW:
Question: Which twentieth century civil rights leaders should I know about?

Answer:

1. Booker T. Washington - c1900 - Believed that African Americans should gradually gain their rights. In the ***Atlanta Compromise***, he told a mostly white audience that African Americans would work with their hands and accept a subservient role in society in exchange for recognition of basic equality and education rights. He became the first head of the Tuskegee Institute in 1881. At the Institute, students gained the skills necessary to succeed as part of the labor force.

2. W.E.B Du Bois - c1920 - Disagreed with Washington's gradual rights ideology. He sponsored the ***Niagara Movement***, which called for desegregation and absolute equality. Remember: **WEB** = **W**ants **E**quality for **B**lacks.

3. Marcus Garvey - c1920 - Leader of the Back to Africa (colonization) Movement that encouraged blacks to return to the land of their ancestry.

4. Rosa Parks - In 1955, Parks refused to give up her seat to a white person on a bus in Montgomery, Alabama. Her arrest inspired blacks to boycott the bus system and protest segregation. The ***Montgomery Bus Boycott*** ended just over a year later when the Supreme Court declared segregation on buses unconstitutional.

5. Martin Luther King, Jr. - c1960 - Becoming a national figure in the Montgomery Bus Boycott, he was outspoken for civil rights. He supported civil disobedience, and passive resistance. He delivered the *I Have a Dream* Speech in 1963 (discussed later).

6. Stokely Carmichael - c1965 - As a leader of the Black Panthers and Black Power movement, he called for immediate civil rights and black separatism. The Black Panther Party was co-founded by Huey Newton and Bobby Seale.

7. Malcolm X - c1962 - A member of the Nation of Islam, he preached black supremacy, and separation of blacks and whites.

8. Freedom Riders - 1961 - Young white and black civil rights advocates rode buses together into the segregated South. They were greeted with violence in Montgomery, Alabama. In Mississippi, riders were arrested for intentionally breaking segregation laws.

9. SNCC (Student Nonviolent Coordinating Committee), and CORE (Congress of Racial Equality) were two organizations comprised mostly of college students. They were involved in many activities including the freedom rides, and ***sit-ins*** (where African Americans deliberately broke Jim Crow laws...see pg. 58) of segregated restaurants.

Definition: Jackie Robinson

On April 15, 1947 Jackie Robinson made his debut for the Brooklyn Dodgers, becoming the first African American to play in a Major

League Baseball game in over sixty years (there were a few African Americans in the game in the 1880s). This triggered a movement to integrate other sports as well.

Definition: *Plessy v. Ferguson,* 1896

To understand segregation, let's go back to 1896. Homer Plessy was part African American, but sat in a white's only railroad car. He was challenging the Separate Car Act of Louisiana which segregated blacks from whites on trains. The Supreme Court decided that "separate but equal" was Constitutional. "Separate but equal" meant that African Americans and whites could be separate, so long as their facilities were the same (which they typically weren't). In the Jim Crow South, that meant separate bathrooms, schools, drinking fountains, and restaurants until about 1954.

Definition: *Brown v. Board of Education of Topeka, Kansas,* 1954

In a landmark case (or really, five cases in one) for ending segregation in schools, a 9-0 decision of the ***Warren Court*** (named for Chief Justice Earl Warren) declared that "separate but equal" was inherently unequal. Thurgood Marshall, later a Supreme Court justice, argued on behalf of Linda Brown and a score of other black children who were denied integration. The NAACP (National Association for the Advancement of Colored People) was instrumental in constructing this case. Although segregation was declared unconstitutional, schools in the South were still voluntarily segregated for years.

Definition: What other court cases of the Warren Court (1953-1969) are important to know?

Answer: Generally speaking, Earl Warren's Court gave ***more rights to the accused***. Details are included for essay purposes:

1. *Miranda v. Arizona,* 1966 - Ernesto Miranda admitted to charges of rape and kidnapping after a lengthy interrogation. Because he did not know that he had a right to remain silent, the Supreme Court ruled that Miranda did not receive fair due process. Since his Fifth Amendment rights were violated, he had to be retried. The controversy of the Warren Court's decision has changed the way police apprehend criminals. Now, a priority is the reading of "Miranda rights" upon arrest. Miranda was later retried and convicted.

2. *Gideon v. Wainwright,* 1963 - Clarence Gideon was accused of breaking into a billiards establishment in Florida. At his trial, he was denied the right to an attorney (he could not afford a lawyer) because Florida only appointed lawyers for capital (murder) offenses. He was found guilty. The Warren Court later ruled that Gideon's rights were violated. His Sixth Amendment rights to a fair trial should have applied to the state of Florida because of the Fourteenth Amendment's due process clause. He was retried and acquitted (found not guilty). Another case, *Escobedo v. Illinois* involved a similar issue.

3. *Mapp v. Ohio,* 1961 - Dollree Mapp's house was searched in Ohio as the police were looking for a fugitive. Instead, they found indecent pornographic material that violated the law. The police seized the evidence and Mapp was convicted. The Supreme Court heard Mapp's appeal, and ruled that the evidence was not admissible in court. This was because the protections of the Fourth Amendment (unreasonable searches and seizures) applied to the states through the Fourteenth Amendment's due process clause.

Definition: Little Rock 9

After the *Brown* decision, controversy rocked

Central High School in Little Rock, Arkansas. The nation's media focused on the violence here when nine students attempting to go to school were met by mobs of protesters. Governor Orval Faubus called in the Arkansas Guard to support segregation. However, President Eisenhower had the final say as Commander-in-Chief of the Army and the chief executer of laws. Ultimately, federal troops enforced integration.

Definition: I Have a Dream Speech, 1963

Martin Luther King, Jr. delivered this landmark speech on August 28, 1963 in Washington, DC. Things to know about the speech:

1. He gave it in front of the Lincoln Memorial, as Lincoln was nicknamed the Great Emancipator.

2. He drew upon the Declaration of Independence, saying that African Americans had been written a "bad check" when it came to the distribution of rights from 1776.

3. He mainly spoke about the hope to see a world free of discrimination, where people of all races could live in harmony.

4. King preached *passive resistance*, or nonviolence. Furthermore, he and his followers practiced *civil disobedience*, or refusing to obey an unjust law.

Definition: Civil Rights Act of 1964

Signed by President Johnson after a lengthy filibuster (delay in vote), this act ended all major forms of discrimination and segregation. Still, civil rights were not absolute in Alabama.

In 1965, SNCC and Southern Christian Leadership Conference members marched from Selma to Montgomery demanding African American voter registration rights. Along the way, they were met with tear gas and violence from Alabama State Troopers.

That year, the **Voting Rights Act of 1965** was passed. This reiterated the wording of the Fifteenth Amendment and prevented discrimination at the polls.

Definition: Kerner Commission

In 1967, race riots broke out in Detroit. Riots had occurred in other Northern cities a year before. President Lyndon Johnson appointed Illinois Governor Otto Kerner, Jr. to get to the bottom of the issues causing the riots. Kerner's Commission offered the opinion that a separate black and white nation was emerging, and measures should be taken to prevent further violence. Months later, rioting would indeed occur all over the North after the assassination of Martin Luther King, Jr.

Definition: George Wallace

George Wallace was a pro-segregation Governor of Alabama. He personally attempted to stop African American students from attending class at the University of Alabama. He was unsuccessful. Wallace ran for President four times, three as a Democrat (never getting the nomination). In 1968 he ran for the far-right American Independence Party. Think: He wanted to put a "wall" up between the races.

History 1960-present

Although the Presidency of Richard Nixon saw an easing of Cold War tensions, there was an increase in tension of his own. His resignation after the Watergate Scandal remains one of the rare events in American History. For his successors, the 1970s saw inflation, unemployment, and high oil prices. In the 1980s, President Ronald Reagan lowered taxes for the wealthy and cut social programs. In the 1990s, President Bill Clinton approved NAFTA, and sent troops into Bosnia. Clinton would also become the second President to be impeached. In the first decade of the 2000s, the War on Terror led to two foreign conflicts in the Middle East.

Definition: Election of 1960 and Television

Richard Nixon used television to save his spot as a Vice Presidential Candidate in 1952. He went on TV to address accusations that he had an illegal money fund as a Senator. Nixon gave his heartwarming *"Checkers Speech"* in which he denied any wrongdoing. In the speech he talked about his dog, Checkers, a campaign contribution whom he was keeping because his kids loved it so much. The speech was a success, and television saved his spot on Eisenhower's ticket.

Television was not good for Nixon in 1960 during his Presidential debates with Democrat John F. Kennedy. Nixon appeared to have won the four debates, but the charisma and charm of the youthful Kennedy may have been more appealing to the voters watching on television. Kennedy won the election.

Question: What should I know about Lyndon B. Johnson's (Democrat) Presidency? (1963-69)

Answer:

1. Inheriting the Presidency after Kennedy was assassinated, Johnson escalated the War in Vietnam via the Gulf of Tonkin Resolution.

2. *The Great Society* was a plan to help the poor, minorities, and the disadvantaged. Johnson declared a *War on Poverty*, and looked to increase education opportunities for all.

3. The monumental Civil Rights Act of 1964 made all forms of segregation and discrimination illegal.

4. In 1965, Medicare became law. This guaranteed health insurance to people over 65 and those with certain disabilities.

5. Johnson did not run for a second full Presidential term as the War in Vietnam tarnished his legacy. After he left office, *The Pentagon Papers*, meant to be secret, were reported by the *New York Times* in 1971. The papers portrayed Johnson's Administration as incapable of handling the Vietnam conflict.

Question: What should I know about Richard Nixon's (Republican) Presidency? (1969-74)

Answer:

1. Nixon exercised détente diplomacy (easing of the tensions between the US and communist powers that existed during the Cold War.)

2. He pulled out of Vietnam in 1973.

3. Extending "ping pong diplomacy" (the US and China had previously set up a series of ping pong matches between the two nations), Nixon visited communist China and Mao Zedong. Some believe this was the beginning of China's industrial boom of today.

4. Congress passed the *War Powers Act*, stating that although the President is Commander-in-Chief, he can't use extensive overseas force (for more than 60 days) without the consent of Congress.

5. Nixon battled inflation in the 1970s.

6. Nixon's Presidency would most be remembered for the Watergate Scandal (explained next).

Definition: Watergate Scandal

During the 1972 Presidential Election campaign, there was a break-in at the Democratic Party headquarters at the Watergate Hotel in Washington, DC. Nixon claimed he knew nothing about it, but taped conversations proved otherwise. After Vice President Spiro Agnew resigned because of income-tax evasion, Nixon would do the same in 1974 to avoid impeachment for *obstruction of justice*.

Definition: Equal Rights Amendment

First proposed in 1923, this amendment that ensured equal rights for women under the law passed both the House and Senate in 1972. The states never ratified it, and it expired in 1982. You need to know:

Betty Friedan was a feminist who wrote *The Feminine Mystique*. She supported equal rights for women, and was the first president of the National Organization for Women (NOW).

Phyllis Schlafly was opposed to modern feminism. She was outspoken against the ERA (Equal Rights Amendment).

So...Betty wanted women to be *FREE* (Friedan), Phyllis wanted to give them the Shaft (Schlafly).

Around the same time, in 1973, the Supreme Court supported a woman's right to choose to have an abortion in the landmark court case of ***Roe v. Wade***. The court ruled that a woman's privacy was protected by the Fourth Amendment, as well as the Ninth Amendment's reservation of rights for the people, and the Fourteenth Amendment's protection of personal liberty.

Question: Besides Friedan and Schlafly, what other famous names should I know about for this era?

1. Rachel Carson's book, *Silent Spring* is important to know. The 1962 book gets a lot of credit for helping to launch the environmental movement that led to the ban of certain pesticides.

2. Andy Warhol - He was a filmmaker, author, and artist. He was most famous for "pop art," where images of pop culture were used in works of art. One of his most famous creations was *Campbell's Soup Cans* in 1962.

3. Ralph Nader - For decades he was a consumer advocate. In 1965, he wrote his most famous book, *Unsafe at Any Speed*, in which he challenged the automotive industry to make safer cars.

4. Benjamin Spock - He was a pediatrician who wrote *The Common Sense Book of Baby and Child Care*, a bestselling book about raising children. Though it was published in 1946, new editions were printed into the 1990s.

5. From the 1960s-1980s, César Chávez of the ***United Farm Workers*** called for boycotts to help farm laborers get better pay and safer working conditions in industries such as grapes and lettuce. (Think "César" Salad!)

Question: What should I know about Gerald Ford's (Republican) Presidency? (1974-77)

Answer:

1. After Spiro Agnew resigned, Ford was appointed to the Vice Presidency prior to Nixon's resignation. When Nixon stepped down, Ford became the first non-elected President (that is, not elected as a President or VP).

2. After taking office, he pardoned (forgiveness of a crime) Nixon. Although this was controversial, Ford believed it was best not to prosecute Nixon so the country could heal.

Question: What should I know about Jimmy Carter's (Democratic) Presidency? (1977-81)

Answer:

1. As a peanut farmer and Governor of Georgia, Carter was a Washington outsider.

2. He battled *stagflation*...high inflation, slow growth, and high unemployment.

3. Carter negotiated the Camp David Accords of 1978, where Egypt agreed to recognize Israel as a nation in exchange for Israel returning the Sinai Peninsula.

4. There was an energy crisis in the 1970s, and rationing of gasoline took place. High energy prices only added to the problems in the economy.

5. In 1979, Iranian students stormed the American Embassy in Tehran, Iran. For 444 days, Americans were held hostage, decreasing morale in the United States, especially after an attempted rescue failed. The hostages were finally released on Ronald Reagan's inauguration day. The crisis coincided with the Iranian Revolution where US ally, Mohammad Reza Pahlavi - the Shah of Iran - was overthrown and Ayatollah Khomeini took power.

6. In 1979, there was a nuclear meltdown at the *Three Mile Island Nuclear Generating Station* in central Pennsylvania. The event led many to question whether nuclear power should be used as an alternative energy source.

Question: What should I know about Ronald Reagan's (Republican) Presidency? (1981-89)

Answer:

1. Reagan increased spending on the military with programs such as the Strategic Defense Initiative, or Star Wars (mentioned earlier). The Soviet Union began to fall apart during his Presidency. As stated earlier, he gave the "tear down this wall" speech in front of the Berlin Wall in 1987.

2. In his economic policy of *Reaganomics*, he supported wealthy businesses so that profits would "trickle down" to all classes. This was related to the *supply-side economics* theory where less government regulation and tax breaks would lead to more investment and job creation. He also cut certain programs to decrease the government's workforce.

3. Like Carter, Reagan was a Washington outsider. He was a former actor and Governor of California.

4. In the 1985 Iran-Contra Affair, senior military officials sold arms to Iran in an attempt to get hostages rescued. In addition, the money from the sale of the weapons was given to Nicaraguan anti-communist rebels known as Contras. Both of the above actions were against American policy.

Question: What should I know about George H.W. Bush's (Republican) Presidency? (1989-1993)

Answer:

1. He was Commander-in-Chief for the Gulf War (Operation Desert Storm) in Iraq where American forces liberated Kuwait from Saddam Hussein.

2. There was a deep economic recession that hurt his re-election campaign.

Question: What should I know about Bill Clinton's (Democratic) Presidency? (1993-2001)

Answer:

1. He favored health-care reform.

2. The economy recovered into prosperity.

3. He sent *NATO troops into Bosnia*, attempting to end ethnic cleansing (genocide).

4. Clinton was impeached by Speaker *Newt Gingrich* and the Republican-controlled House of Representatives for *obstruction of justice*. He lied about doing something naughty with

an intern in the White House. He was not convicted by the Senate.

5. He negotiated The North American Free Trade Agreement *(NAFTA)* that lifted certain tariffs between the US, Mexico, and Canada.

6. In 1993, the official policy towards homosexuals in the military became "***don't ask, don't tell***." It allowed gay and lesbian soldiers to serve, as long as they kept their sexual orientation a secret.

7. The *Brady Bill* led to more background checks for owning firearms.

Question: What should I know about George W. Bush's (Republican) Presidency? (2001-2009)

Answer:

1. Despite losing the popular vote in 2000, he won the electoral vote in a disputed election where the Democrats contended that not every vote was properly counted.

2. After the US was attacked by terrorists on 9/11/2001, he led the military efforts in the War on Terror to remove both the Taliban from power in Afghanistan, and Saddam Hussein from Iraq.

3. The War on Terror necessitated the creation of the ***Department of Homeland Security***. This agency looks to keep Americans safe from terrorist activity.

4. Bush signed the ***Patriot Act***, which gave law enforcement more power to search, gather information, deport, or detain suspected terrorists.

5. He left office amidst a recession.

Question: What should I know about Barack Obama's (Democrat) Presidency? (2009-present)

Answer:

1. Obama was the first African American to win the Presidency.

2. Taking the Presidency during a recession, he promoted stimulus bills that aimed to fix the economy.

3. He favored universal healthcare.

4. He supported an end to "don't ask, don't tell" in the military. This now meant that anyone, regardless of sexual orientation, could openly serve in the military without fear of being discharged.

5. An increase in the national debt occurred during his first few years of office.

6. Ten years after the 9/11 attacks, al-Qaeda's Osama bin Laden was killed by American forces in Pakistan.

Review Questions

1. All of the following were true about *Brown v. Board of Education* EXCEPT:
   A) It was a unanimous decision
   B) The case was argued by Thurgood Marshall
   C) It was the first time the Supreme Court heard a case on Jim Crow
   D) The court found that separate but equal was inherently unequal
   E) The decision was controversial in many areas, as there was not always peaceful integration

2. Unlike Martin Luther King, Jr., Black Panther Stokely Carmichael
   A) demanded equal rights for African Americans
   B) advocated for black separation
   C) stood by the Atlanta Compromise formulated by Booker T. Washington
   D) believed African Americans should be able to vote without interrogation
   E) demanded reparations for the sharecropping era

3. A major goal of Lyndon B. Johnson's Great Society was to
   A) socialize the American healthcare system
   B) eliminate poverty through education and vocational training
   C) expand the welfare system to pregnant mothers
   D) end social programs to compensate for lower taxes
   E) promote discrimination in private industry

4. The Warren Court's decision in *Miranda v. Arizona*
   A) expanded rights to accused individuals
   B) limited free speech
   C) expanded the right to bear arms
   D) ended the period of prohibition
   E) gave cops more power in reasonable searches and seizures

5. Which of the following describes the ideas of Martin Luther King, Jr.?
   A) Financial reparations for all citizens who were the children of former slaves
   B) De facto, or voluntary segregation of the races
   C) Using force to achieve African American equality
   D) Disobeying unjust laws of segregation
   E) Encouraging mass northern migrations of African Americans from the South

6. Richard Nixon and Bill Clinton were both targeted for
   A) abusing their powers as Commander-in-Chief
   B) obstruction of justice
   C) pardoning of war criminals
   D) taking bribes while in office
   E) not equipping NATO troops

7. The kidnapping of hostages at the Iranian Embassy and a spike in oil prices were associated with which twentieth century President?
   A) Ronald Reagan
   B) Gerald Ford
   C) Richard Nixon
   D) Dwight Eisenhower
   E) Jimmy Carter

8. The first President of the National Organization for Women was
   A) Betty Friedan
   B) Phyllis Schlafly
   C) Hillary Clinton
   D) Jane Addams
   E) Elizabeth Cady Stanton

9. The Camp David Accords led to
   A) embargo of all Middle Eastern oil
   B) peace between the nations of Egypt and Israel
   C) release of American hostages from Iran
   D) decrease in oil output by OPEC
   E) demilitarization of the Sinai Peninsula

10. Ronald Reagan's policies of *Reaganomics*
    A) created a vast amount of social welfare programs
    B) increased the power of labor unions
    C) decreased spending on the military
    D) pumped money into education endeavors
    E) decreased taxes on the wealthy

Answers and Explanations

1. **C**. This was not the first challenge to Jim Crow. There were others, including *Plessy v. Ferguson* way back in 1896.

2. **B**. Carmichael was a member of the Black Panthers. He spoke out for separation.

3. **B**. Johnson's Great Society aimed to help the poor and increase educational opportunities.

4. **A**. Miranda admitted to a rape, but did not know he had a right to remain silent. In a controversial decision, his conviction was overturned because of a Fifth Amendment (due process) violation.

5. **D**. Dr. King wanted to end segregation and integrate all people. He was an advocate for passive resistance and civil disobedience.

6. **B**. Both were targeted for obstruction of justice, or lying. Nixon about Watergate, and Clinton about a relationship with an intern.

7. **E**. These events happened during the Carter Administration. Carter attempted to send a rescue mission for the hostages, but one of the helicopters crashed. The hostages were held a total of 444 days and released when Ronald Reagan was inaugurated.

8. **A**. Betty Friedan was an advocate for the Equal Rights Amendment that never passed. Phyllis Schafly was against the amendment.

9. **B**. After fighting several wars, Israel and Egypt pledged peace. This was an accomplishment for Jimmy Carter.

10. **E**. In "trickle down" economic theory, tax breaks on the rich should eventually benefit the poor.

Breakdown of the Tests

In case you want to know the breakdown of each test, here it is. We don't recommend looking too much into these numbers. You shouldn't change your study habits based on a percentage.

On the AP United States History Exam's multiple choice, you will have 55 minutes to complete 80 questions.

Time Periods:
Pre-Columbian to Constitutional Convention - 20%
Washington to Before World War I - 45%
Post World War I to Modern Day - 35%

Material Covered:
Political and Public Policy - 35%
Social and Cultural - 40%
Foreign Policy - 15%
Economics - 10%

You will then have one hour to write a Document Based Question Essay.

Parts B and C of the test will ask you to write 2 out of 4 essays in 70 minutes. (Essays will be explained later).

The test is scored out of 5, with a 3 counting as a passing grade.

On the SAT Subject Test you will have 60 minutes to complete 90 questions. There are no essays.

Time Periods:
Pre-Columbian History to 1789 - 20%
1790 to 1898 - 40%
1898 to Present - 40%

Material Covered:
Political History - 31-35%
Economic History - 13-17%
Social History - 20-24%
Intellectual and Cultural History - 13-17%
Foreign Policy - 13-17%

The test is graded out of 800 points.

No Bull Tips for AP Exam and SAT Subject Test Multiple Choice

No Bull Disclaimer: Students are always looking to get an edge. But sometimes, they do pretty well just by their own abilities. We don't recommend changing your style drastically if you are scoring well.

In this section, we will give advice to those who have trouble finishing the test on time.

Here are five tips to help you finish your test strongly in the allotted time constraint:

No Bull Tip #1, You're on the Clock

Wear a watch, take a clock.

When you have 80-90 questions to answer in an hour, things can get tough. That's why you don't have to just know your stuff, but you have to be able to answer multiple choice questions with some degree of speed. ***On the AP and SAT Subject Tests, you will find some questions noticeably easier than others.*** We recommend that you breeze through these at a good clip. No more than 30 seconds per question. 30 Seconds should be more than enough time for a question you find easy.

Specifically, give yourself enough time for **EXCEPT** questions. These tend to take a longer time to answer. Typically, when students answer these hastily, they make an error. Here, we recommend taking 45 seconds. If you time yourself properly, you should be done with question 50 after about half an hour. If you look at your watch and see you have taken more time to do 50 questions, then quicken the pace. If you are too leisurely with your time, you will not finish either test.

No Bull Tip #2, Be Careful on Centuries

"Nineteenth century"...Cross it out! People don't think in terms of centuries, they think in terms of years. Some of the questions might say: *In the early nineteenth century...* Cross out "early nineteenth century," and write down 1800-1820...Make "mid-twentieth century" 1950-1960. Oftentimes, students get confused as to which time-period the question is referring to. This eats up precious time! As honor students, you are very smart. But, you are still human. Don't be 100 years off because of a simple mistake. Cross it out.

No Bull Tip #3, Know When to Omit

If you are stuck on a question, don't stare it at for an eternity. Here's our guide for guessing:

Luckily, for the AP Exam, life got better in 2011 because there is no longer an omit option. So, on the AP Exam, answer ***everything***. On the SAT Subject Test, here is the rule of thumb: ***Play the probability***. If you can eliminate two of the five choices, then by all means, answer the question. Percentagewise, you would have to have the worst luck on the planet to not at least break even.

For every question you get wrong, you lose 1/4 of a point. So, if you have 3 choices to choose from, your odds are now 1 in 3...if you can get down to two choices, it's 1 in 2. If you are correct 1 out of every 3 guesses, you come out ahead. If you get just 1 out of every 4 guesses right, you break even. If you are looking to get a high score, then you cannot afford to omit too many questions. If you get a question about someone who you've never heard of, that's when you should omit. There's a list of all people you may never have heard of on the No Bull Review Sheet. ***But*** *if you are looking to get a grade higher than 700, you better not omit too many.*

No Bull Tip #4, Skip the Long Passages, For Now

We recommend this tip for people who struggle with the time constraint. If questions have difficult graphs or long passages to read, then answer them last. They are time consuming, and are only worth one question. You could do five questions in the same time it takes to read one long passage.

If you follow this strategy, and you do run out of time, it's as if you only omitted a few questions... rather than half of the test.

BEWARE though: Make sure you skip the choice on your answer sheet, as to not mess up your answer order. If time is *not* a factor for you, then we recommend answering the test in normal sequence.

No Bull Tip #5, Bubble in Your Answers NOW!

On most tests, it is recommended to circle an answer on the test, and then go back over each question before bubbling in your answer-sheet. This is risky business on the AP Exam and SAT Subject Tests.

This again depends on how you are as a test taker. It could take you over 5 minutes to bubble in an answer sheet after a test. You might not have that much time.

Every year there are students who should have received a 5 on a test, yet received a 3 because they didn't bubble in 20 or more answers. To be safe, time yourself doing a practice test and see how things go.

No Bull Essay Review

The SAT Subject Test has no essay section. The AP United States History Exam has two sections of essays, or Free-Response Questions. All essay questions for the last decade of tests are available online. They are not a secret.

The first section, Part A, is a ***Document Based Questions*** (DBQ) essay. The test will give you a series of about ten documents (A through I, J, or K). It is your job to group these documents into different categories, and argue a thesis.

By now, your teacher should have showed you a long rubric illustrating how the DBQ is scored. We are here to trim the fat out of that long rubric. You will do great on the DBQ if you answer yes to the following:

1. Did I put the documents into proper groups?
2. Did I include the right information from the documents?
3. Did I use all of the documents?
4. Do I have a detailed thesis?
5. Is my outside information impressive?
6. Did I write with *exhaustive breadth*?
7. Did I prove my thesis?

Let's assume we have a DBQ that offers the following question:

1. How did the social, economic, and political controversies of the antebellum period create disunion by 1861?

No Bull Tip #1, Grouping Documents

Every DBQ sets up a task that will divide documents into different groups. Read the question first, and then make a grid that looks like this:

Document Letter

Social	
Economic	
Political	

As you go through each document, put its letter in the proper place on the grid. Let's assume that your documents are as follows:

A. An excerpt from William Lloyd Garrison's *The Liberator*.

B. A speech from Stephen Douglas calling for popular sovereignty in the states.

C. Roger B. Taney's decision of the *Dred Scott* case.

D. A graph showing the profits of the cotton trade in the South.

E. A Boston newspaper advertisement warning free blacks about the Fugitive Slave Act.

F. A map showing the expansion of railroads and canals. The map shows how in 1830 there were similar numbers of railroads and canals in the North and South. But by 1860, the North has greatly outpaced the South.

G. A passage from Harriet Beecher Stowe's *Uncle Tom's Cabin*.

H. A letter from a South Carolina cotton plantation owner defending the existence of slavery.

I. An excerpt from the *South Carolina Exposition and Protest* that affirms the rights of the states.

J. A soldier's journal from the bombing of Fort Sumter.

After flipping through the documents, you have determined that your grid now looks like this:

Document Letter

Social	**A, E, G**
Economic	**D, F, H**
Political	**B, C, I**

But what about **Document J**? Sometimes you might think that one of the documents doesn't fit. No, it does. If it doesn't fit…you make it fit! **Get out a shoehorn and make it fit!** In your introduction or last body paragraph, say: "With all of the sectional problems, it was inevitable that Fort Sumter was bombed in April of 1861 to start the Civil War." Then, you can talk about Document J a bit. Sometimes a document will go against your thesis. In that case you say the following: "Yes, what Document K says negatively about the New Deal is true to some degree, however mostly, the New Deal was a success because of…"

Note: When citing documents, you can either say: "In Document A, Garrison says…," or you can just put (Doc. A) at the end of the sentence.

Now the essay will come in well-organized paragraphs.

No Bull Tip #2, What to Include From the Documents

The DBQ is a trap! It gives you way too much information to read if you are going to write a long essay. So, it is best for you to scan the document. Mark that thing up! Include only bits and pieces of it. You need to know the main idea, point of view, and bias of the document more so than every little detail within. Since you have your watch at the testing site, spend no more than two minutes per document. That's right! Put yourself on the clock. In those two minutes you should be able to write down in the margin of each document the answers to the following:

1. What is this about?
2. Where does it fit in my essay?
3. Who is writing this, and what is their bias or point of view?
4. What outside information can I use for this? (explained below)

About two minutes per document will give you roughly forty minutes to write the actual essay. But since you have done the bulk of the organization beforehand, the essay will basically write itself.

No Bull Tip #3, You Better Have a Strong Thesis

The test wants you to make a thesis. Be warned! Do not just use the sentence they give you as the thesis. We know that there are economic, political, and social causes of the war. If you get a little creative, it will help your grade.

Average Thesis: The economic, political, and social issues of the antebellum period created a division between North and South that eventually led to the Civil War.

Better Thesis: Because the South was economically dependent on the plantation system, political and social divisions began to divide the nation.

The second thesis shows a greater level of creative and critical thinking. If you can go the extra mile, then do so. If not, that's OK, just try to make it up with your outside information.

Tip #4, Exhaustive Outside Information

No Bull, you need to have a lot of outside information. As you go through each document, jot down notes in the margins. Your documents should be drowning in ink by the end of the hour! Include anything...ANYTHING...relevant that isn't in the documents. For example, Document E deals with the Fugitive Slave Act. In the margin write down *"Comp. of 1850,"* *"Missouri Comp before that, 36° 30'."* Any note about the slave compromises would be a great addition of outside information.

I don't see anything about secession in the documents. That's outside information.

I don't see anything about the election of Abraham Lincoln. That's outside information.

I don't see John Brown or Harper's Ferry. That's outside information.

Throw it all in. You need *exhaustive breadth,* or a great scope of knowledge, to get the highest grade. It's all about what you put into your sentences.

Normal Breadth: The Fugitive Slave Act was a part of the Compromise of 1850, which was controversial.

Exhaustive Breadth: The Compromise of 1850, designed at first as an omnibus by "The Great Compromiser" Henry Clay, but passed as separate bills with the help of "The Little Giant" Stephen Douglas, provided for a strict Fugitive Slave Act.

Normal Breadth: Stephen Douglas delivered the Freeport Doctrine in the Lincoln-Douglas Debates.

Exhaustive Breadth: Democrat Stephen Douglas' Freeport Doctrine, that affirmed popular sovereignty, was delivered in the 1858 Illinois Senatorial Debate between him and Republican candidate Abraham Lincoln.

Do you see the difference? Throw in a fact here, a year there. That's exhaustive breadth!

Typically, the DBQ will be on a broad topic that's not impossible to write about.

Here are some of the topics used over the last decade:

1. Manifest Destiny.
2. The Cold War in the 1950s.
3. The American Revolution's affect on social, political, and economic life.
4. The Vietnam War's impact on social, political, and economic life.
5. Slavery from the colonial period to before the Civil War.

Again, all DBQs given in the last decade are available online.

Parts B and C: The Scary Essays

Don't be scared about Parts B and C. It's true…there are no documents to use as crutches. *It really comes down to studying the right material.* That's what we will talk about regarding the Part B and C essays below.

Much like the DBQ, the AP Test historically asks questions about major themes. It's fair in that respect. You should **_not_** see:

1. Give the causes and effects of the Aroostook War.
2. Explain how Rutherford B. Hayes' religion impacted his Presidency.

That would just be unfair. The biggest tip for Parts B and C is…to study the right material! A huge pitfall for students is that in May, they try to go back and read their textbook cover to cover. No Bull! You are wasting your time! You need to know the important concepts. Don't go back and attempt to remember every provision of the Treaty of Ghent. Instead, study the themes below. They are the ones more likely to come up on Parts B and C of the test.

What You Should Study The Most

1. Social History. That means, know stuff about slavery, religious movements, immigration, minorities, and women.
2. Liberal reform movements. Know how Populism grew into Progressivism. Also, how Progressive ideas could be seen in New Deal legislation.
3. Civil War causes and the slave compromises.
4. Reconstruction legislation and how it was ignored during Home Rule in the South.
5. The Age of Jackson/Age of Reform.
6. Causes of the American Revolution, and an end to salutary neglect.

These are the items to study. Sure, there could be a Cold War or modern Presidential essay. But, if one should come up, your teacher probably taught it to you recently. Therefore, you should remember that information from class. If your teacher did not get up to that material, read through the *No Bull Review Sheet Recent Presidents Section*. Here is how a sample Part B and C essay might look. Again, all of the real essays from the last decade are available online.

Part B

2. Explain how the ideas of the Omaha Platform of 1892 affected TWO of the following from 1900-1935:

Participation in politics
Business reform
Help for the farmer

3. Explain how the Second Great Awakening inspired social movements of TWO of the following from 1830-1850:

Women's rights
Abolition
Utopian communities
Temperance

Part C

4. Analyze the success of Reconstruction by discussing life in the 1890s for African Americans regarding TWO of the following:

Universal suffrage
Equal rights
Economic prosperity

5. Explain Britain's policies concerning TWO of the following after the end of salutary neglect:

Taxation
Rights to property
Representation
Settlement of territories

100 More Practice Questions

1. Thomas Paine's *Common Sense*
   A) condoned revolutions in France after the rise of the Jacobins
   B) said that a small island should not control a large continent thousands of miles away
   C) believed that citizens of the colonies had certain unalienable rights that could not be denied
   D) agreed that a monarchy could survive, but only if consent of the governed was reflected
   E) stated that only Parliament could legislate for the colonies, not the King

2. The British enacted the Stamp Act in 1765 which
   A) was an internal tax on tea
   B) extended Parliamentary rule over the lands west of the Appalachian Mountains
   C) made it mandatory for soldiers to reside in private homes
   D) taxed legal and other paper documents
   E) increased the price of sugar imports

3. Which of the following was true of the Northwest Ordinance of 1787?
   A) The land was received in the Louisiana Purchase
   B) Slavery was banned in the territory
   C) It was overridden by the Webster-Ashburton Treaty
   D) Texas was annexed peacefully after its issuance
   E) France refused to listen to it, and continued to populate the Oregon trail

4. All are true of the Constitution's Great Compromise EXCEPT:
   A) It created a bicameral legislature
   B) The compromise is still in effect today
   C) It gave equal representation to states within the House of Representatives
   D) New Jersey's plan, part of the compromise, provided for equal representation
   E) The Virginia Plan was favored by the more populous states

5. Which legislative idea of the seventeenth century became a model for the current United States Congress?
   A) House of Burgesses
   B) Mayflower Compact
   C) New England Town Meetings
   D) House of Commons
   E) Joint-stock company hierarchy

6. The purpose of the Bill of Rights was to
   A) appease the Federalists who refused to ratify the Constitution
   B) emphasize the importance of protecting individual rights in the Constitution
   C) guarantee the right to vote to all citizens
   D) increase the power of the Executive Branch
   E) apply the rights of the Constitution to both men and women

7. The Virginia and Kentucky Resolutions can be compared to what other writing of the mid-nineteenth century?
   A) *South Carolina Exposition and Protest*
   B) Jackson's Bank Veto
   C) *The Federalist*
   D) *The Liberator*
   E) *The Impending Crisis of the South*

138

8. Which of the following called for America to be economically self-sufficient in the first half of the nineteenth century?

A) James Monroe's Doctrine
B) Henry Clay's American System
C) Andrew Jackson's Spoils System
D) Abraham Lincoln's House Divided speech
E) John C. Calhoun's *South Carolina Exposition and Protest*

9. What action of Andrew Jackson led to a split in political parties in 1832?

A) Force Bill
B) Indian Removal Act
C) Veto of the Bank of the United States
D) Signing of the Tariff of 1832
E) Spoils System

10. The Seneca Falls Convention of 1848

A) was the first ever formal gathering held for abolition
B) led to a Women's Declaration of Sentiments
C) brought Unitarians and Mennonites together for religious compromise
D) promoted the thoughts of Charles Grandison Finney
E) illustrated the importance of domestic manufacturing

11. The Second Great Awakening directly influenced the

A) utopian community at Brook Farm
B) Equal Rights Amendment
C) Lowell Factory system
D) settlement house movement
E) removal of Native Americans to reservations

12. Horace Mann of Massachusetts was best known for his

A) incorporation of women in reform movements
B) literature for the abolition of slavery
C) religious revivals in the "burned over district" of upstate New York
D) promotion of a public education system
E) creation of the modern day American factory system

13. The Wilmot Proviso of 1846 called for

A) Washington, DC to end the practice of trading slaves
B) an end to the expansion of slavery into certain territories
C) nullification of the Tariff of Abominations
D) annexation of Texas as a slave state
E) Missouri to enter the union as a slave state

14. The Compromise of 1850 provided for

A) popular sovereignty in Kansas, but not Nebraska
B) Missouri to enter the Union as a slave state
C) an outlaw of all slavery north of the 36° 30' line
D) Maine to become a free state
E) a strict fugitive slave act

15. John Brown and Nat Turner were similar in that both

A) supported states' rights
B) led unsuccessful slave rebellions
C) protested against the Tariff of Abominations
D) ran as a third party candidate in a Presidential Election
E) were opponents of the spoils system

Use the map below to answer questions 16 and 17.

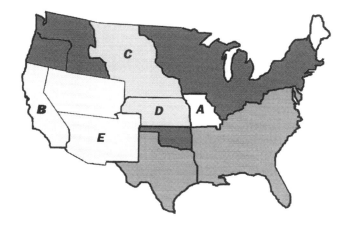

16. Space "A" became a slave state after the
   A) Missouri Compromise
   B) Kansas-Nebraska Act
   C) Compromise of 1850
   D) Dred Scott Decision
   E) Northwest Ordinance

17. The Lecompton Constitution would be approved to allow slavery in
   A) A
   B) B
   C) C
   D) D
   E) E

18. All of the following regarding slaves in the Civil War were true EXCEPT:
   A) Many were confiscated as contraband by the Union Army
   B) Black Regiments were formed in the North
   C) Slaves who were freed in the border states after the Emancipation Proclamation flocked to the Union army
   D) Many slaves remained loyal to their masters in the South and helped with the Confederate war-effort
   E) The Confederacy threatened to kill any black soldier, or Union officer of a black regiment, caught in the war.

19. How did Presidential Reconstruction differ from Radical Reconstruction?
   A) Presidents Lincoln and Johnson wanted to treat the South as conquered territory
   B) Radical Republicans supported a 10% oath
   C) Both the Presidents and Radical Republicans wanted to be lenient to the South
   D) Radical Republicans supported military rule to enforce legislation
   E) Both the Presidents and Radical Republicans believed that former Confederate office holders should be banned from serving in government for life

20. After the end of Reconstruction in 1877, the Southern Redeemers did all of the following EXCEPT:
   A) Instituted the Mississippi Plan to intimidate black voters
   B) Promoted the use of literacy tests
   C) Supported Jim Crow legislation
   D) Did not obey the Thirteenth Amendment
   E) Charged a poll tax to make it harder for blacks to vote

21. *"In bestowing charity, the main consideration should be to help those who will help themselves; to provide part of the means by which those who desire to improve may do so; to give those who desire to use the aids by which they may rise; to assist, but rarely or never to do all."*

Which robber-baron was most associated with this quote?
A) Andrew Carnegie
B) John D. Rockefeller
C) Cornelius Vanderbilt
D) Jay Gould
E) James Fisk

22. All of the following were true of political machines and municipal bosses of the late nineteenth century EXCEPT:
A) They aimed to racially integrate government offices
B) They were often corrupt and took money from the public
C) Voter fraud was common, as people voted "early and often"
D) Immigrants were provided with jobs, or money, in exchange for votes
E) They tended to exist in urban areas

23. Most immigrants in the Second (New) Wave of immigration of the late nineteenth century-early twentieth century settled in
A) cities in the North
B) Midwestern farm states
C) rural areas west of the Mississippi
D) Canada
E) Southeastern industrial states

24. *"Silver, which has been accepted as coin since the dawn of history has been demonetized to add to the purchasing power of gold by decreasing the value of all forms of property as well as human labor, and the supply of currency is purposely abridged to fatten usurers, bankrupt enterprise and enslave industries."*

The above debate was discussed as part of
A) *The Jungle*
B) The Omaha Platform
C) Hepburn Act
D) The Sherman Anti-Trust Act
E) The Federal Reserve Act

25. How did Theodore Roosevelt's handling of the Anthracite Coal Strike of 1902 compare to Grover Cleveland's actions during the Pullman Strike of 1894?
A) Both used force to break up the strike
B) Cleveland sided with the employees
C) Both Presidents sided with the employers
D) Whereas Cleveland broke up the strike, Roosevelt sided with the workers
E) Roosevelt and Cleveland let the strikes play out in the name of laissez-faire

26. All of the following were aims of the Progressive Era of the early twentieth century EXCEPT:
A) Cleaning up the abuses of the Gilded Age
B) Bringing more government to the people
C) Narrowing the gap between the rich and poor
D) Providing social reform to those in need
E) Elimination of the closed-shop union

27. The New South refers to
A) the end to segregation after 1954
B) a repeal of the literacy test
C) an increase in Jim Crow laws
D) creation of industry after Reconstruction
E) the rise of the Ku Klux Klan

28. The goal of the Open Door Policy was to
A) allow all immigrants to enter the United States, regardless of their country of origin
B) trade with Britain before World War II, despite the desire for neutrality
C) protect United States trade in China
D) prevent railroads from securing a monopoly
E) allow all citizens the right to take advantage of nominating conventions

29. The Gentlemen's Agreement of 1907 limited immigration from
A) China
B) Japan
C) Poland
D) Russia
E) Britain

30. During the New Deal, the Supreme Court
A) approved of economic, but not the political issues of Franklin Roosevelt
B) declared several key acts unconstitutional
C) supported Congress and the President in all forms of legislation
D) declared Social Security unconstitutional
E) was increased from nine seats, to fourteen

31. During both World War I and World War II, American women
A) fought overseas
B) became isolated in their homes
C) entered factories to fill jobs left vacant by men fighting abroad
D) demanded equal pay for equal work in the private sector
E) unionized to gain greater wages and rights through strikes

32. American foreign policy in the second half of the twentieth century can best be described as
A) imperialism in the Caribbean
B) containment in Europe and Asia
C) noninvolvement
D) Dollar Diplomacy in China
E) support for nuclear proliferation in the Middle East

33. The actions of the House Un-American Activities Committee and Senator Joseph McCarthy were similar in that both
A) advocated for a policy of détente
B) were against the execution of the Rosenbergs
C) condoned the deployment of nuclear weapons
D) believed treasonous government officials should be targeted
E) supported an invasion of the Soviet Union

34. Which of the following books would be an example of nonconformity in the Beat Generation?
A) Jack Kerouac - *On the Road*
B) Rachel Carson - *Silent Spring*
C) Jacob Riis - *How the Other Half Lives*
D) Ralph Nader - *Unsafe at Any Speed*
E) Benjamin Spock – *The Common Sense Book of Baby and Child Care*

35. President Eisenhower's Administration created the
    A) Marshall Plan
    B) plan for interstate highways
    C) Mars rover
    D) Peace Corps
    E) Federal Reserve

36. The 1964 escalation of the war in Vietnam was a result of the
    A) Domino Theory of Dwight Eisenhower
    B) Gulf of Tonkin Resolution
    C) Nixon Doctrine
    D) Eisenhower Doctrine
    E) Tet Offensive

37. Richard Nixon's policy of Vietnamization called for
    A) a gradual reduction of the reliance on US ground troops in Vietnam
    B) an end to the policy of using napalm in the war
    C) a surrendering of forces after the Tet Offensive
    D) expansion of the draft
    E) the United Nations to invade Cambodia and Laos

38. George Wallace was best known for his ideas of
    A) taking a more open approach about limiting nuclear weapons with the Soviet Union
    B) reintroducing segregationist ideas to the South
    C) ending the War in Vietnam
    D) increasing educational opportunities for minority students
    E) removing government officials loyal to the Communist Party

39. Which of the following best describes the ideas of SNCC and CORE?
    A) Reparations for all citizens who were the children of former slaves
    B) Disobeying unjust laws of segregation
    C) Using force to achieve African American equality
    D) De facto, or voluntary, segregation of the races
    E) Mass northern migration of African Americans from the South

40. The Presidency of Jimmy Carter of the late 1970s involved all of the following EXCEPT:
    A) High prices on oil
    B) Conflict in the Middle East
    C) Stagflation
    D) Shortage of energy supplies
    E) Vietnam War protests

41. Modern Day environmentalism was influenced by which author?
    A) Jacob Riis
    B) Rachel Carson
    C) Betty Friedan
    D) Jack Kerouac
    E) Sinclair Lewis

42. The decisions of the Warren Court in the middle of the twentieth century were best known for
    A) expanding rights of the accused
    B) limiting free speech
    C) segregating the South
    D) eliminating the powers of corporate trusts
    E) depriving the civil liberties of Japanese Americans

43. The demonstrations and massacre at Kent State University were related to

A) segregation

B) the broadening of civil rights

C) labor protests for greater union rights and collective bargaining

D) discontent with the Vietnam War

E) strong support for an Equal Rights Amendment

44. Richard Nixon's Administration saw all of the following occur EXCEPT:

A) The end to the Vietnam War

B) His impeachment

C) SALT Treaty

D) A visit to China

E) Moon landing

45. Which of the following pushed for the creation of the Equal Rights Amendment?

A) Phyllis Schlafly

B) Betty Friedan

C) Elizabeth Cady Stanton

D) Susan B. Anthony

E) Lucretia Mott

46. Presidents Ronald Reagan and Jimmy Carter were similar in that both

A) attempted the rescue of American hostages from Iran

B) supported a policy of détente

C) were not part of Washington, DC politics before being elected

D) supported the theory of "trickle down" economics

E) negotiated treaties between Israel and Egypt

47. Which of the following is paired with the proper writing?

A) Phyllis Schlafly -*The Feminine Mystique*

B) Rachel Carson - *On The Road*

C) Angelina Grimké - *An Appeal to the Christian Women on the South*

D) Jacob Riis - *The Jungle*

E) Harriet Beecher Stowe - *The Liberator*

48. Where would the influence of the Zenger trial decision be seen in the Bill of Rights?

A) The First Amendment which protects freedom of the press

B) The Fourth Amendment that protects against unreasonable searches and seizures

C) The Tenth Amendment which addresses division of powers

D) The Eighth Amendment that protects against cruel and unusual punishment

E) The Third Amendment which protects against the quartering of troops

49. Why did the English monarchy establish a rule of salutary neglect in the American colonies?

A) Agricultural dominance in the South meant an abandonment of mercantilist policies

B) The Great Awakening caused the King to intervene on behalf of the Church

C) Britain was economically satisfied, so they looked the other way on certain social and political affairs

D) The House of Burgesses was permitted to operate so long as a bicameral legislature was present

E) The English Bill of Rights was not applicable to overseas colonies

50. All of the following were results of the French and Indian War EXCEPT:

A) The removal of the Spanish from North America

B) The end of France as a major power in the 13 colonies

C) The emergence of George Washington as a recognizable name in the colonies

D) The need for Britain to raise money to support their army

E) An end to salutary neglect

51. *"The power to tax involves the power to destroy"*

The above quote is most associated with what Supreme Court decision by John Marshall?

A) *Marbury v. Madison*

B) *Gibbons v. Ogden*

C) *McCulloch v. Maryland*

D) *Worcester v. Georgia*

E) *Dartmouth v. Woodward*

52. Henry David Thoreau and Ralph Waldo Emerson were most associated with

A) higher tariffs to protect American jobs

B) a reliance on nature and peace

C) a state of perfection which would lead to a millennium

D) a "city upon a hill"

E) breaking up monopolies

53. All of the following were associated with abolitionism EXCEPT:

A) William Lloyd Garrison

B) Angelina Grimké

C) Harriet Beecher Stowe

D) John Brown

E) Stephen Douglas

54. The Haymarket Affair and Taft-Hartley Act were similar in that both

A) led to increases in nativism

B) limited the power of labor unions

C) favored poor laborers

D) illustrated the need for suffrage reform

E) occurred during the Gilded Age

55. In the Freeport Doctrine, Stephen Douglas affirmed his belief that

A) Blacks should not own property

B) Slavery should not expand to newly formed states in the west

C) All territories gained in the Mexican War should be closed to slavery

D) Popular sovereignty should be favored over the Dred Scott decision

E) States should be able to declare acts of Congress "null and void"

56. The spark that led to the secession of the Southern states was the

A) Compromise of 1850

B) Dred Scott decision

C) Harper's Ferry slave rebellion

D) violence of Bleeding Kansas

E) election of Abraham Lincoln

57. Which of the following acts that provided for popular sovereignty were passed in the antebellum period?

A) Missouri Compromise

B) Kansas Nebraska Act

C) Ostend Manifesto

D) Fugitive Slave Act

E) Wilmot Proviso

58. All of the following were examples of nativism EXCEPT:

A) Red Scare
B) Emergency Quota Act
C) Sacco-Vanzetti Case
D) Molly Maguires
E) Roosevelt Corollary

59. Andrew Mellon's views in the 1920s supported

A) promotion of jazz music
B) tax breaks for the wealthy
C) the emergence of the flapper
D) an end to prohibition
E) citizenship rights for Native Americans

60. *Plessy v. Ferguson* affirmed which of the following?

A) Separate but equal was constitutional
B) The Civil Rights Act of 1866 was unconstitutional
C) Jim Crow laws were unconstitutional
D) Schools in Kansas could be segregated with the consent of the people
E) The Due Process clause of the Fourteenth Amendment made all segregation unconstitutional

61. Booker T. Washington's Atlanta Compromise called for

A) an immediate end to Jim Crow
B) anti-lynching legislation
C) a hope for gradual freedom and equality
D) the integration of schools
E) an end to the poll tax

62. All of the following are paired with the proper author EXCEPT:

A) Rachel Carson - *Silent Spring*
B) Harriet Beecher Stowe - *Uncle Tom's Cabin*
C) Frederick Jackson Turner - *Common Sense*
D) William Lloyd Garrison - *The Liberator*
E) Jack Kerouac - *On the Road*

63. All of the following were leaders of slave rebellions EXCEPT:

A) Denmark Vesey
B) John Brown
C) Nat Turner
D) Frederick Douglass
E) Toussaint L'Ouverture

64. Folk singers of the late 1960s such as Phil Ochs and Tom Paxton mostly disagreed with which of the following actions of President Johnson?

A) Medicare
B) The Great Society
C) Escalation of the war in Vietnam
D) Gun Control Act
E) War on Poverty

65. The majority of workers in the Lowell Factory System in 1835 were

A) married men
B) Russian immigrants
C) young women
D) German immigrants
E) slaves

66. All of the following were parts of the Omaha Platform of 1892 EXCEPT:

A) A secret ballot

B) Direct election of United States Senators

C) A graduated income tax

D) The raising of tariffs to support big business

E) Free and unlimited coinage of silver at a rate of 16:1 with gold

67. Legislation regarding immigration in the 1920s looked to

A) increase the number of immigrants to fill unskilled jobs

B) end immigration from all countries in Western Europe

C) increase the amount of immigration coming from Asia

D) limit immigration from Southern and Eastern Europe

E) close America's doors to future immigration from the Western Hemisphere

68. Which event led to the resignation of Richard Nixon?

A) The tax-evasion scandal of his Vice President

B) Failure to end the War in Vietnam

C) Accusations of obstruction of justice

D) Illegally taking money out of a campaign fund

E) Refusal to give up gifts given to his campaign

69. In the early nineteenth century, the American Colonization Society wanted to

A) provide "40 acres and a mule" to all newly freed slaves

B) send freed slaves to Liberia in Africa

C) establish a policy of sharecropping

D) support the settlement of western lands by African Americans

E) encourage newly freed slaves to migrate to the North

70. Andrew Jackson did not admit Texas into the Union because

A) Texas would disrupt the balance of free and slave states

B) any admission of Texas would incite Spain into fighting a war

C) Santa Anna had reclaimed Texas as part of Mexico

D) parts of Texas north of the Rio Grande were still under dispute

E) Texas had refused to pay the Tariff of 1828

71. The immediate reaction of the US Government after the Soviet launch of Sputnik in 1957 was

A) the sending of aid to West Berlin

B) an increase in spending on American education and technology

C) a moon launch later that same year

D) the execution of Americans who gave the Soviets information on rockets

E) deployment of missiles to Turkey

72. *"There would be meat stored in great piles in rooms; and the water from leaky roofs would drip over it, and thousands of rats would race about on it. It was too dark in these storage places to see well, but a man could run his hand over these piles of meat and sweep off handfuls of the dried dung of rats."*

The above quote could be found in

A) *The Impending Crisis of the South* by Hinton Rowan Helper

B) *How the Other Half Lives* by Jacob Riis

C) *The Jungle* by Upton Sinclair

D) *On the Road* by Jack Kerouac

E) *Silent Spring* by Rachel Carson

73. George Washington set a precedent on foreign policy by advocating

A) imperialistic opportunities in the Western Hemisphere

B) annexation of land in the Pacific northwest

C) avoiding alliances with foreign nations

D) protecting American naval rights in the Mediterranean

E) removal of Native Americans to west of the Mississippi River

74. Which of the following was inspired by Keynesian economics?

A) Tax on whiskey

B) Smoot-Hawley Tariff

C) New Deal deficit spending

D) Re-charter of the Bank of the United States

E) Creation of the Federal Reserve

75. Which political party was formed to protest Harry Truman's stance on Civil Rights?

A) Dixiecrat

B) Whig

C) Know-Nothing

D) Green

E) Independent

76. Which event was partially responsible for the United States declaring war on Spain in 1898?

A) Interception of the Zimmermann Telegram

B) Unrestricted submarine warfare in the Atlantic

C) Platt Amendment

D) Sinking of the USS *Maine*

E) The Panamanian Revolution

77. As a Presidential candidate, Abraham Lincoln believed that slavery

A) should be abolished in the border states

B) could be abolished in states added after 1800

C) could stay where it was, but not expand to new states in the west

D) should be abolished everywhere in the US

E) was protected in the Constitution, and could not be deprived

78. After John Marshall's decision in *Worcester v. Georgia*, President Andrew Jackson

A) stopped the removal of all Native Americans

B) ignored Marshall's recommendations

C) reworded the Indian Removal Act for Congressional approval

D) allowed Cherokees to return to their land

E) secured the land of New Mexico as a future Native American Reservation

79. Alexander Hamilton's national bank was passed
    A) with the help of the Elastic Clause
    B) after a joint session of Congress and the Supreme Court
    C) as a compromise which moved the nation's capital to New York
    D) as part of the Treaty of Paris
    E) after an override of President Washington's veto

80. The Pendleton Act of 1883 was successful in ending
    A) unrestricted submarine warfare
    B) the patronage system of appointing supporters to office
    C) unionization of workers after the Haymarket Affair
    D) the gold standard as a means of backing the US currency
    E) European colonization of nations in the Western Hemisphere

81. In its first years, the Sherman Anti-Trust Act was used mostly to
    A) destroy monopolies
    B) break up unions
    C) remove Native Americans to reservations
    D) put an end to unfair campaign funding
    E) set quotas on immigration

82. In the first few decades of the seventeenth century, the Chesapeake Bay area was an agricultural center where
    A) slaves harvested cotton
    B) Native Americans planted rice
    C) indentured servants farmed tobacco
    D) free blacks planted sugar
    E) individual families farmed self-sufficiently

83. Which of the following was true of women with regard to the right to vote before 1920?
    A) They could not vote
    B) Some states allowed them to vote in different types of elections
    C) All women could vote in Presidential elections
    D) Southern states allowed women to vote in all elections
    E) If women passed a federal literacy test, they could vote in all elections

84. After the Boston Tea Party of 1773, Britain implemented the
    A) Sugar Act
    B) Tea Act
    C) Declaratory Act
    D) Townshend Acts
    E) Intolerable Acts

85. All of the following were causes of the War of 1812 EXCEPT:
    A) American nationalism
    B) Continued impressment of American sailors on the high seas
    C) A desire to acquire parts of Canada
    D) Malcontent with Britain after the *Chesapeake-Leopard* Affair
    E) A territorial dispute on the Maine-Canadian border

86. Which of the following best defends the idea of Social Darwinism in the late nineteenth century?
    A) The decision of the Scopes Trial
    B) Existence of monopolies
    C) Use of the spoils system
    D) Completion of the Transcontinental Railroad
    E) The Bessemer process

87. *"...we will answer their demand for a gold standard by saying to them: You shall not press down upon the brow of labor this crown of thorns, you shall not crucify mankind upon a cross of gold."*

The above was said

A) before the outbreak of World War I

B) in response to the Roosevelt Corollary

C) during the Presidential Campaign of 1896

D) after the Populist Era, but before the Progressive Era

E) in the last days of Woodrow Wilson's Presidency

88. In its decision of *Korematsu v. United States*, the Supreme Court

A) limited civilian Constitutional rights in a time of war

B) extended the belief that the protections of the Fourteenth Amendment were absolute

C) stated that free speech was not absolute

D) declared that persons naturalized in America were citizens

E) illustrated that a state could not deprive someone of their right to an attorney

89. The Dawes Severalty Act of 1887

A) was passed to give reparations after the Wounded Knee massacre

B) offered citizenship and land in exchange for abandoning aspects of tribal culture

C) promised free land to African Americans in accordance with the Homestead Act

D) was declared unconstitutional by the Supreme Court

E) decreased the need for industry in the South

90. The United States did not join the League of Nations or ratify the Treaty of Versailles because

A) they refused to keep Germany divided after World War I

B) there were reservations to the idea of making firm alliances with foreign nations

C) the United States did not want to donate troops to the League of Nations army

D) France and Germany had not signed the treaty

E) the home of the League of Nations would be located in New York

91. Traditionally before World War I, the Republican Party attracted all of the following voters EXCEPT:

A) Northern industrialists

B) Southern African Americans

C) Wall Street executives

D) Immigrants in urban areas

E) Robber barons of the railroads

92. In *Marbury v. Madison*, Chief Justice John Marshall

A) used the principle of judicial review

B) upheld the constitutionality of the Judiciary Act of 1789

C) voiced strong misgivings to the creation of a national bank

D) denied states the right to make contracts

E) struck down a fraudulent purchase of land near the Yazoo River

93. Unlike Thomas Jefferson, Alexander Hamilton believed

A) in a loose interpretation of the Constitution, and use of the Elastic Clause
B) that a strong army would deprive citizens of their rights
C) the educated commoner should rule
D) the US should support France in accordance with the alliance of 1778
E) a strong government would threaten states' rights

94. Discontent over the gap between the rich and the poor could be seen in which colonial event?

A) Bacon's Rebellion
B) Salem Witch Trials
C) King Philip's War
D) Pequot War
E) Great Awakening

95. In Federalist #10, James Madison argued that

A) a large republic could never successfully exist
B) the Electoral College would protect the voting rights of all
C) tyranny of factions could be controlled in a large republic
D) the Articles of Confederation could succeed if there was a stronger army
E) all men were created equal with unalienable rights

96. Which of the following was a result of the eighteenth century Great Awakening?

A) Increase in the number of Quakers in Rhode Island
B) Creation of the halfway covenant
C) Increase in religious practice
D) Creation of the colony of Rhode Island
E) A decrease in Presbyterians

97. In John Marshall's decision of *Gibbons v. Ogden*, the court ruled that

A) separate but equal was inherently unequal
B) the federal government was supreme to the states
C) the national bank was constitutional
D) slavery could not expand to west of the Mississippi
E) tribal land grants had to go through the federal government

98. All of the following women were associated with the suffrage movement EXCEPT:

A) Susan B. Anthony
B) Mary Chapman Catt
C) Jane Addams
D) Lucy Stone
E) Elizabeth Cady Stanton

99. Social society during the Presidency of Dwight Eisenhower was best characterized as a time period where

A) women questioned traditional morals

B) there was a decrease in marriage

C) public education was reserved for the rich

D) conformity and moves to suburbia were quite common

E) an easing of Cold War tensions led to an influx of Russian immigrants

100. The "graying" of America has led to problems with the

A) Federal Deposit Insurance Corporation

B) Social Security fund

C) Reconstruction Finance Corporation

D) National Defense fund

E) Federal Emergency Relief Administration

Answers and Explanations

1. **B**. Thomas Paine believed that it was "common sense" for America to be independent from Britain, as it was miles away and larger.

2. **D**. The Stamp Act was a direct tax on all paper materials and legal documents.

3. **B**. The Northwest Ordinance provided for the admission of new states, which would be free of slavery.

4. **C**. The House of Representatives is based on population. The states with a greater population have more representatives. The Senate has equal representation.

5. **A**. The House of Burgesses was a representative assembly in Virginia. The House of Representatives created by the Constitution provides for a similar representative government.

6. **B**. The Bill of Rights, added in 1791, was an appeal to Anti-Federalists who believed the Constitution would infringe upon individual rights. The Bill of Rights came after the Constitution was ratified.

7. **A**. John C. Calhoun's *South Carolina Exposition and Protest* said that states should be able to declare acts of Congress "null and void." This was similar to what Thomas Jefferson and James Madison wrote in 1798-99 in their Virginia and Kentucky Resolutions.

8. **B**. Henry Clay believed the US could be economically self-sufficient. He supported higher tariffs, a bank, and internal improvements with infrastructure projects like bridges and roads.

9. **C**. Issues with the national bank caused the first two major party splits in American History. The split in the 1830s led to the formation of the Whig Party.

10. **B**. Women drafted a Declaration of Sentiments at the convention, and stated that men and women were created equal.

11. **A**. The Second Great Awakening led to education reform, temperance, abolition, and utopian communities. The utopian community at Brook Farm was one of these. You should also know the name Robert Owen for New Harmony, Indiana. Both looked to create a perfect society based on communal work. And both lasted less than a decade.

12. **D**. "Mann, did he love public education." In the late 1830s, Horace Mann promoted public schools in Massachusetts. The movement spread to other states during the Second Great Awakening/Age of Reform.

13. **B**. David Wilmot's Proviso (stipulation) said that no slavery should spread to lands that might be acquired in the War with Mexico. The Proviso never became law, but it put the slave issue on the table. Soon after, a Northern Free-Soil Party would emerge.

14. **E**. The Fugitive Slave Act in the Compromise of 1850 provided for the capture and return of runaway slaves.

15. **B**. John Brown (1859) and Nat Turner (1831) led failed slave rebellions.

16. **A**. Space A is showing the state of Missouri, which became a slave state in 1820.

17. **D**. The Lecompton Constitution approved slavery for the state of Kansas. "Bleeding Kansas" was a violent series of events that occurred during the process of popular sovereignty stemming from the Kansas-Nebraska Act.

18. **C**. The Emancipation Proclamation did not free any slaves in the northern or border states that were loyal to the Union. It only "freed" slaves in the rebelling states who did not listen to federal law.

19. **D**. Highlighted by the Reconstruction Acts of 1867, Radical Republicans favored military rule to enforce legislation.

20. **D**. The Thirteenth Amendment abolished slavery. This was never in question after Reconstruction.

21. **A**. Andrew Carnegie is explaining the "Gospel of Wealth," or the idea that robber barons like himself should be charitable with their fortune and help those who wish to rise to prominence.

22. **A**. Political bosses like Boss Tweed of Tammany Hall were not concerned with racial integration. The other choices were all associated with political machines. Political bosses were known for municipal (city) corruption.

23. **A**. Immigrants moved to cities because that's where the jobs were.

24. **B**. Silver, or a 16:1 ratio of silver to gold, has to do with the Populists' Omaha Platform of 1892.

25. **D**. Theodore Roosevelt said he gave those coal miners a "square deal" by making employers accept arbitration. Cleveland broke up the Pullman Strike in 1894.

26. **E**. Closed shops were not eliminated until the 1947 Taft-Hartley Act. A closed shop meant that one could not work a job unless they were in a specific union.

27. **D**. The New South has nothing to do with race or Jim Crow. It meant an increase in industry for the late nineteenth century agrarian South. Cheap land and resources made industry an appealing alternative there.

28. **C**. Because John Hay wanted to protect American interests in China, he declared it open to all foreign trade. European nations had carved China into spheres of influence, or areas of imperialistic control.

29. **B**. The Gentlemen's Agreement was between the US and Japan. It restricted emigration from Japan to the United States.

30. **B**. Congress and the President were on the same page, but not the Supreme Court. *Schechter Poultry Corporation v. US* led to the end of the National Industrial Recovery Act. *US v. Butler* struck down the Agricultural Adjustment Act.

31. **C**. Women helped out first during World War I. They received the right to vote at the end of the war. Rosie the Riveter was the name for women who worked in the factories during World War II.

32. **B**. From 1945-1991, America's foreign policy was to stop the spread of communism. This was known as containment.

33. **D**. Both HUAC and McCarthy looked to remove suspected communists. This turned into a witch-hunt, oftentimes with faulty evidence leading to convictions.

34. **A**. Jack Kerouac's *On The Road* is typically the most important book to know regarding Beatnik writings. Beat Generation members were non-conformists who renounced materialism and modern society in the 1950s.

35. **B**. After World War II, there was a great move to the suburbs. The Federal-Aid Highway Act of 1956 created the modern day interstate highway system.

36. **B**. The Gulf of Tonkin Resolution gave President Johnson a "blank check" as Commander-in-chief of the Vietnam conflict. This meant an escalation of the use of ground troops.

37. **A**. Nixon's policy aimed to give control of the war to Vietnamese soldiers in South Vietnam.

38. **B**. Governor Wallace of Alabama ran for President several times as a segregationist candidate from the South.

39. **B**. SNCC (Student Nonviolent Coordinating Committee), and CORE (Congress of Racial Equality) were two civil rights organizations involved in many activities including the freedom rides and sit-ins.

40. **E**. The Vietnam War ended in 1973 under President Nixon.

41. **B**. Rachel Carson's 1962 book, *Silent Spring* is about environmentalism, and led to the banning of certain pesticides.

42. **A**. Earl Warren expanded the rights of the accused in court decisions such as *Miranda v. Arizona*, *Gideon v. Wainwright*, and *Mapp v. Ohio*.

43. **D**. In 1970, four students were shot and killed while they were protesting the Vietnam War at Kent State University in Ohio.

44. **B**. Nixon was never impeached. He resigned before he could be impeached for obstruction of justice associated with the Watergate Scandal.

45. **B**. Betty Friedan was a feminist leader who supported the Equal Rights Amendment. She wanted women to be "Freeeee idan." Choice A, Phyllis Schlafly wanted the opposite. She wanted women to be in a traditional role. You might say, she wanted to give women the shaft (or schlaft).

46. **C**. Carter was a peanut farmer and Governor of Georgia, and Reagan was an actor and Governor of California. Voters usually see Washington outsiders as a welcome change to "politics as usual."

47. **C**. Angelina Grimké appealed to women to support abolition.

48. **A**. The Zenger decision said that if something is true, then it can't be libel (crime for printing false claims). Zenger was a journalist, and the decision helped establish freedom of the press.

49. **C**. Salutary neglect took place at a time when the profiting British Government did not enforce trade laws extensively. They also let their guard down on social and political movements in the colonies. Salutary neglect ended after the French and Indian War.

50. **A**. Spain remained in places like Mexico. This included parts of the modern day west coast of the United States.

51. **C**. John Marshall's decisions generally increased the power of the federal government. For example, in *McCulloch v. Maryland*, he said that Maryland could not tax the Bank of the US.

52. **B**. Transcendentalist philosophy meant embracing nature, renouncing materialism, and finding inner peace.

53. **E**. Don't get your Douglases confused. Frederick Douglass (2 S's, African American) was for abolition. Stephen Douglas (1 S, white) championed popular sovereignty, or the right for territories to choose to have slavery or not.

54. **B**. In 1886, a bomb went off in Haymarket Square in Chicago. Unions were blamed and labeled as anarchists. Union membership declined. The Taft-Hartley Act took away some union rights in 1947. Notably, closed shops were outlawed. A closed shop meant that one had to be in a union to work a certain job.

55. **D**. Douglas defended popular sovereignty, or the right of people in a territory to choose if they would have slavery or not. He believed it to be more binding to the states than Roger Taney's decision in the Dred Scott case that said slave ownership could not be denied. The Freeport Doctrine was explained in a speech during the 1858 Lincoln-Douglas debates.

56. **E**. Lincoln was a Republican. The Republican Party was viewed by the South as a threat to slavery. South Carolina seceded in 1860, followed by the rest of the Confederacy.

57. **B**. Though the concept of popular sovereignty existed before 1854, the Kansas Nebraska Act would be its most famous application. The passage of the act would lead to Bleeding Kansas.

58. **E**. Nativism meant a fear of foreigners or immigrants. The Roosevelt Corollary was a foreign policy statement, not related to nativism.

59. **B**. Mellon was a Republican Secretary of the Treasury in the 20s. With that knowledge, you can figure out that he wanted to give tax breaks to the wealthy. Try to remember that "Republicans ate a lot of Mellon back then."

60. **A**. *Plessy v. Ferguson* is the opposite of *Brown v. Board of Education*. In *Plessy*, "separate but equal" was seen as constitutional. This meant that as long as blacks and whites had the same type of facilities, they could be separate. *Brown* reversed that in 1954.

61. **C**. Washington's speech was criticized by civil rights leaders like W.E.B. Du Bois. Du Bois, and his Niagara Movement, believed African Americans should receive immediate rights of equality. Washington wanted to gradually gain freedoms, while being subservient to whites in political affairs.

62. **C**. Frederick Jackson Turner wrote a thesis about the frontier. *Common Sense* was written by Thomas Paine during the American Revolution.

63. **D**. Frederick Douglass was an abolitionist who looked to end slavery by conventional means, not violence. His slave narrative was widely read in the North.

64. **C.** The Gulf of Tonkin Resolution escalated the War in Vietnam, and led to deployment of more troops. This upset many of the folk singers and the young generation of draftees who listened to them.

65. **C.** Young women, or mill girls, worked in Lowell, Massachusetts. After the first Great Wave of Immigration of the 1840s, many Irish immigrants took over.

66. **D.** The Populists were similar to Democrats in that they did not want to raise tariffs so businesses could get stronger.

67. **D.** In the 1920s, it was believed that immigrants from Southern and Eastern Europe were inferior to those from Western Europe. A pseudoscience called eugenics fueled these beliefs. Quotas were created to limit immigrants seen as "undesirable."

68. **C.** Nixon lied about what he knew about the Watergate Scandal. He was targeted for obstruction of justice, but resigned before he could be impeached.

69. **B.** Many, including Abraham Lincoln for a time, believed that African Americans should be sent back to their continent of ancestry. The American Colonization Society was an odd mix of abolitionists, politicians, and slave owners who were afraid of having impoverished freed slaves nearby.

70. **A.** Jackson did not want to annex Texas because it would have opened up a can of worms concerning the slave state vs. free state imbalance. Texas would be annexed as a slave state in 1845 by President Tyler.

71. **B.** After being embarrassed by the superior technology of the Soviets, the United States stepped up funding for education and scientific research. In 1969, the US won the race to the moon.

72. **C.** Rats, dangerous working conditions, or something disgusting means the passage is from *The Jungle*. The book led to the Meat Inspection Act and the Pure Food and Drug Act (which created the Food and Drug Administration).

73. **C.** Washington wanted to isolate the US, and avoid foreign alliances. The belief was that the United States was too fragile a nation to meddle greatly in foreign affairs.

74. **C.** Deficit spending ideas came from British economist John Maynard Keynes. To raise revenue, the government can sell bonds and raise taxes.

75. **A.** The Dixiecrat Party (States' Rights Democratic Party) was a short-lived segregationist political party that split from the Democrats in 1948 when Harry Truman integrated the military.

76. **D.** We now know that the *Maine* sank on its own. In 1898, the event was blamed on the detonation of a Spanish mine.

77. **C.** You need to know that Lincoln was against the spread of slavery, and was not an abolitionist in 1860.

78. **B.** Jackson did not listen to Marshall when he said that Georgia could not pass laws regarding Cherokee lands. Jackson said, "John Marshall has made his decision, now let him enforce it."

79. **A**. The Elastic Clause allows Congress – and only Congress – to do anything "necessary and proper." Be warned, Thomas Jefferson never used the clause when purchasing Louisiana. He used implied powers, or loose interpretation of the Constitution, and made a treaty with France for the purchase.

80. **B**. The patronage system was synonymous with the spoils system where elected officials appointed their supporters and friends to government jobs. This ended in 1883 when the Pendleton Act was passed. The act was created after an angry office seeker assassinated President James Garfield in 1881.

81. **B**. This is one of the hardest questions in the 100. If you got it right, great work. Originally, the Sherman Anti-Trust Act was used to bust unions, not monopolies. In 1914, the Clayton Anti-Trust Act clarified the language of the Sherman Act.

82. **C**. The Chesapeake Bay area of Maryland and Virginia was populated by indentured servants who harvested tobacco for the Virginia Company.

83. **B**. A common misconception is that women could not vote before the Nineteenth Amendment was ratified in 1920. Women could vote in certain states, including Wyoming which was the first. Typically, it was the low populated western states that allowed women to vote. Some states only allowed them to vote in Presidential elections.

84. **E**. The Intolerable, or Coercive, Acts of 1774 punished the colonies by closing down Boston Harbor and making them pay for the destroyed tea. In addition, a new quartering act was put in place that allowed troops to stay in the homes of citizens. The Quebec Act was also passed, which expanded the Roman Catholic region of Quebec, which the predominantly Protestant colonists were against.

85. **E**. The dispute over the Maine-Canadian border occurred years later in the nonviolent Aroostook War. Daniel Webster negotiated the Webster-Ashburton Treaty that ended the conflict.

86. **B**. Social Darwinism was used to defend the existence of monopolies. The belief was that "survival of the fittest" would exist in business, similar to what would happen in nature according to Charles Darwin.

87. **C**. William Jennings Bryan of the Democrats and Populist Party favored silver in the money supply. He lost the Election of 1896 to Republican William McKinley.

88. **A**. Executive Order 9066 gave the government the power to round up Japanese Americans, and relocate them to internment camps during World War II. The Supreme Court agreed that these actions were justified in a time of war. The decision showed the limits of the Fourteenth Amendment, as Japanese Americans were not given the same rights as other ethnic groups.

89. **B**. The goal of the Dawes Act was to assimilate Native Americans. Land and citizenship were offered in return. The deal wasn't so good, as the land had to be lived on for 25 years before ownership. Also, whites claimed some of the best pieces of land.

90. **B**. Senator Henry Cabot Lodge had "Lodge Reservations" to joining the League, because it would violate neutrality rights of America. If you said choice C, sorry...the League had no army. The United Nations would have one after World War II.

91. **D**. Immigrants in urban areas typically voted Democratic. This was especially true in New York City where the Tammany Hall political machine flourished.

92. **A**. Judicial review gives the Supreme Court the power to declare an act of the Legislative or Executive Branch unconstitutional. Marshall used it for the first time in this 1803 case.

93. **A**. Hamilton wanted a strong central government which would have flexibility in creating laws to meet the needs of the people.

94. **A**. Bacon's Rebellion saw Nathaniel Bacon leading discontented indentured servants against the wealthy planter class and the governor. King Philip (Metacom), and the Pequot War were conflicts between colonists and Native Americans. The other choices involved religion.

95. **C**. Madison contended that factions, or groups of individuals with special interests, would be kept in check.

96. **C**. The Great Awakening was a religious revival that spread throughout the northern colonies. It was the first true mass-movement in colonial history. The American Revolution would spread to all of the colonies a few decades later.

97. **B**. In this case, Marshall ruled that a ferry license given by the federal government superseded one given by the State of New York. Because business was being done between New York and New Jersey, it was Congress's job to regulate such interstate commerce. Marshall generally upheld the supremacy of the federal government.

98. **C**. Jane Addams was known for her work at Hull House in Chicago, a settlement house which aided poor immigrants in the late nineteenth century.

99. **D**. The Baby Boom began after World War II. Generally, women returned to the home to raise children. There was an exodus from the cities into the suburbs. In addition, many moved to the "sunbelt" to live in the American South and Southwest.

100. **B**. "Graying" means getting older. As people live longer and healthier lives, there will be problems paying out Social Security. Social Security was designed as a pension fund to help the elderly during the Great Depression. As life expectancy has increased since the 1930s, these payments have become increasingly harder to make.

Scoring Guide

Note: This is not scientific.

AP Exam Scoring Guide

Each question is worth one point, no deductions. Note, this is only a multiple choice score, and does not factor in essay grades.

78 - 100 – 5
66 - 77 – 4
54 - 65 – 3
37 - 53 – 2
 0 - 36 – 1

SAT Subject Test Scoring Guide

Get your raw score by first adding the total questions correct. Then for every four wrong, subtract a point off of your raw score.

91 -100 – 800
87 - 90 – 790
84 - 86 – 780
82 - 83 – 770
80 - 81 – 760
78 - 79 – 750
76 - 77 – 740
74 - 75 – 730
72 - 73 – 720
70 - 71 – 710
68 - 69 – 700
66 - 67 – 690
64 - 65 – 680
62 - 63 – 670

60 - 61 – 660
58 - 59 – 650
56 - 57 – 640
54 - 55 – 630
52 - 53 – 620
50 - 51 – 610
48 - 49 – 600
46 - 47 – 590
44 - 45 – 580
42 - 43 – 570
40 - 41 – 560
38 - 39 – 550
36 - 37 – 540
34 - 35 – 530
32 - 33 – 520
31 – 510
30 – 500
29 – 490
28 – 480
27 – 470
26 – 460
25 – 450
24 – 440
23 – 430
22 – 420
21 – 410
20 – 400
19 – 380
18 – 360
17 – 340
16 – 320
15 – 300

Now we're ready to begin!

NO BULL
~~NOBLE~~ **REVIEW SHEET**

Here are my Review Sheets. Use them often to help you study.

You will notice numbers in brackets after a word or paragraph. These are the pages where you can find more detailed information.

Good luck!

Your friend,

Nobley

Most Important Terms of the Course

1. Indentured Servant [5]
2. Bacon's Rebellion [5]
3. Zenger Trial [6]
4. Mayflower Compact [7]
5. Separatists [5]
6. City Upon a Hill [5]
7. Salutary Neglect [7]
8. Metacom (King Philip) [6]
9. Middle Passage [6-7]
10. Stono Rebellion [7]
11. House of Burgesses [7]
12. Great Awakening [6]
13. Halfway Covenant [5-6]
14. Fundamental Orders of Connecticut [7]
15. Albany Plan of Union [8]
16. French and Indian War [8]
17. Mercantilism [7]
18. Navigation Acts [7]
19. Proclamation of 1763 [12]
20. Stamp Act [12]
21. Townshend Acts [12]
22. Boston Massacre [12]
23. Committees of Correspondence [13]
24. Boston Tea Party [13]
25. Intolerable Acts [13]
26. *Common Sense* [14]
27. Continental Congress [14]
28. Olive Branch Petition [14]
29. Declaration of Independence [14]
30. Battle of Saratoga [14]
31. Republican Motherhood [15]
32. Articles of Confederation [15]
33. Land Ordinances [16]
34. Shays' Rebellion [15-16]
35. Philadelphia Convention [16]
36. Federalists & Anti-Federalists [16-17]
37. Federalist Papers [17]
38. Federalist #10 [17]
39. Great Compromise [16]
40. 3/5 Compromise [16]
41. Commercial Compromise [16]
42. Elastic Clause [18, 22]
43. Bill of Rights [17]
44. Whiskey Rebellion [24]
45. Jay Treaty [24]
46. Pinckney Treaty [24]
47. Proclamation of Neutrality [24]
48. XYZ Affair [24]
49. Alien and Sedition Acts [24]
50. Virginia and Kentucky Resolutions [25]
51. Louisiana Purchase [25]
52. Judicial Review [26]
53. Embargo Act [26]
54. The *Chesapeake* [26]
55. Hartford Convention [27]
56. American System [28]
57. Monroe Doctrine [28]
58. Corrupt Bargain [32-33]
59. Sectionalism [32]
60. Spoils System [33]
61. Caucus & Nominating Conventions [33]
62. Jacksonian Democracy [33]
63. Alexis deTocqueville [33]
64. Tariff of Abominations [35]
65. *South Carolina Expostion & Protest* [35]
66. Ordinance of Nullification [35]
67. Indian Removal Act [36]
68. Trail of Tears [36]
69. Second Great Awakening [37]
70. Transcendentalism [37]
71. Mormons [38]
72. Seneca Falls Convention [37]
73. Temperance [37]
74. Hudson River School [38]
75. Brook Farm [38]
76. Abolitionism [46]
77. Missouri Compromise [42]
78. Manifest Destiny [43]
79. Wilmot Proviso [44]
80. Compromise of 1850 [44]
81. Kansas-Nebraska Act [44-45]
82. Bleeding Kansas [45]
83. Lecompton Constitution [45]
84. Republican Party [46]
85. *Dred Scott* Case [46]
86. Lincoln-Douglas Debates [46-47]
87. John Brown [47]
88. Election of 1860 [47]
89. Secession [47]
90. Anaconda Plan [52]
91. Emancipation Proclamation [53]
92. Civil War Draft [53-54]
93. Homestead Act [68]
94. Black Codes [56]
95. Freedmen's Bureau [56]
96. Impeachment of Andrew Johnson [57]

97. Reconstruction Acts of 1867 [57]
98. Carpetbaggers and Scalawags [57]
99. Ku Klux Klan [57]
100. Literacy Tests [58]
101. Jim Crow Laws [58]
102. Sharecropping [58]
103. Home Rule [58]
104. New South [58]
105. Nativism and Immigration Quotas [66-67]
106. Robber Barons and Trusts [63]
107. Social Darwinism and Edward Bellamy [63]
108. Gospel of Wealth [63]
109. Transcontinental Railroad [66, 68]
110. Knights of Labor [64]
111. AFL [64]
112. IWW [64]
113. Pendleton Act [64]
114. Railroad Strike of 1877 [65]
115. Pullman Strike [65]
116. Haymarket Affair [65]
117. Sherman Anti-Trust Act [66]
118. Granger Movement [73]
119. Dawes Severalty Act [68]
120. Wounded Knee [69]
121. Roosevelt Corollary [84]
122. Big Stick Diplomacy [84]
123. Panama Canal [84]
124. Teller and Platt Amendments [84]
125. Open Door Policy [84]
126. Conservation [76]
127. Triangle Shirtwaist Fire [76]
128. Election of 1912 [77]
129. Underwood Tariff [77]
130. FTC [77]
131. Red Scare [86]
132. Lost Generation [90]
133. Flapper [90]
134. Sacco-Vanzetti [91]
135. Great Migration [90]
136. Harlem Renaissance [91]
137. Teapot Dome Scandal [91-92]
138. Scopes Trial [91]
139. Dust Bowl [92-93]
140. Bonus Army [93]
141. Reconstruction Finance Corporation [92]
142. Smoot-Hawley Tariff [92]
143. Fireside Chats and Keynesian Economics [97]
144. AAA [98]
145. NIRA [99]
146. SEC [98]

147. Court Packing [99]
148. Wagner Act [99]
149. Lend Lease Act [104]
150. Good Neighbor Policy [104]
151. Yalta Conference [105]
152. Atomic bombs [105]
153. GI Bill [107]
154. Taft-Hartley Act [107]
155. United Nations [107]
156. Containment [111]
157. Truman Doctrine [112]
158. Marshall Plan [112]
159. Berlin Airlift [112]
160. NATO [112]
161. Sputnik [112]
162. McCarthyism [112]
163. Domino Theory [115]
164. The Rosenbergs [112]
165. U-2 [112-113]
166. Election of 1960 [123]
167. Bay of Pigs Invasion [114]
168. Cuban Missile Crisis [114]
169. Gulf of Tonkin Resolution [115-116]
170. Tet Offensive [116]
171. Beatniks and Hippies [107, 116]
172. Détente [114]
173. Nixon Doctrine [116]
174. Little Rock 9 [121-122]
175. Civil Rights Act of 1964/Voting Rights Act of 1965 [122]
176. War Powers Act [123]
177. Watergate [124]
178. Stagflation [125]
179. Camp David Accords [125]
180. César Chávez [124]
181. Iran Hostage Crisis [125]
182. Reaganomics [125]
183. Iran-Contra Affair [125]
184. Equal Rights Amendment [124]
185. *Silent Spring* [124]
186. Operation Desert Storm [125]
187. North American Free Trade Agreement [125]
188. Election of 2000 [126]

Know these terms and you will find success.

Key Questions

1. What were the causes of the American Revolution? [13]

2. What were the weaknesses of the Articles of Confederation? [15]

3. What were the precedents and foreign policy of George Washington? [22, 24]

4. Describe the aspects of Hamilton's financial plan. [22-23]

5. What were the causes and results of the War of 1812? [26-27]

6. Why did Andrew Jackson veto the Bank of the US? What happened to the economy after the veto? [34]

7. What economic changes occurred during the market revolution c1830? [33-34]

8. What were some of the effects of the Second Great Awakening on Reform Movements? [37]

9. What should I know about slavery? [42]

10. What were the causes of the Civil War? [47-48]

11. What was Lincoln fighting for at the beginning of the Civil War? [52]

12. How did black troops make an impact in the Civil War? [53]

13. How did Presidential Reconstruction differ from Radical Reconstruction? [56]

14. Why did Reconstruction end? [57-58]

15. What were the two Great Waves of immigration? [66]

16. What were the causes and results of the Spanish-American War? [83-84]

17. What did the Populists want? [73]

18. How did Populist ideas become Progressive Era reforms? [74]

19. What were the reforms of the Progressive Era? [78]

20. What muckrakers do I need to know about? [76]

21. What famous women reformers of the Progressive Era should I know about? [78-79]

22. What was Theodore Roosevelt's stance on both trusts, and labor? [75-76]

23. Why did the US maintain a foreign policy of imperialism in the late nineteenth century? [83]

24. Why didn't the US ratify the Treaty of Versailles? [85-86]

25. What were the causes of the Great Depression? [92]

26. What programs did FDR create to help the unemployed? [98-99]

27. How did the Supreme Court respond to the New Deal? [99]

28. Why did Truman order the dropping of the Atomic Bomb? [105]

29. Who were the most important civil rights leaders? [120]

30. What were major examples of containment during the Cold War? [113]

Constitutional Compromises

The Great Compromise

Virginia Plan (bicameral based on population) vs. New Jersey Plan (equal representation). The Compromise provided for a two-house (bicameral) legislature where the House of Representatives is based on population, and the Senate has equal representation (2 Senators per state).

3/5 Compromise

Slaves counted as 3/5th of a white person for both taxation and representation.

Commercial Compromise

Imports shall be taxed with a tariff, exports will not be taxed. Tariffs are "customs duties."

Amendments to Know

Including the Bill of Rights, you need to know the following Amendments. Remember: The Bill of Rights was ratified in 1791, two years after the Constitution went into effect. Of the ten, these are the most important to know:

Bill of Rights Amendments (1791)

1st – Freedoms of speech, press, religion, assembly, and right to petition the government.
2nd – Right to bear arms.
4th – Freedom from unreasonable searches and seizures.
5th – Due process rights (right to fair justice, and freedoms from self incrimination). Also, one cannot be tried twice for the same crime. This is a freedom from "double-jeopardy."
6th – Right to a fair trial and attorney.
10th – Division of power between the states and federal government (called federalism).

Civil War Amendments

13th Amendment (1865) – Abolition of Slavery [56]
14th Amendment (1868) – Equality [56]
15th Amendment (1870) – Universal Male Suffrage [56]

Progressive Era Amendments

16th Amendment (1913) – Graduated Income Tax [74-75]
17th Amendment (1913) – Direct Election of Senators [75]
18th Amendment (1919) – Prohibition…Was it successful? [77-78, 91]
19th Amendment (1920) – Women's Suffrage [79]

Other Important Amendments

22nd Amendment (1951) – Two Term Limit for Presidents [106]
26th Amendment (1971) – Lowered the voting age to 18 in 1971, as Vietnam War soldiers were not old enough to vote [116]

Supreme Court Cases — A Short Synopsis

Marbury v. Madison (1803) - First use of judicial review. [26]

McCulloch v. Maryland (1819) - Maryland could not tax the Bank of the United States because of federal supremacy, and the right of the national government to charter a bank. [This, and other Marshall Court decisions are found on pg. 28.]

Worcester v. Georgia (1832) - The Supreme Court ruled that Georgia could not pass legislation regarding Cherokee land. [36]

Dred Scott v. Sandford (1857) - Chief Justice Roger B. Taney said that slaves were property, and owners could not be deprived of them. [46]

Slaughterhouse Cases (1873) - The Fourteenth Amendment did not protect slaughterhouse workers attempting to conduct a business. [59]

Plessy v. Ferguson (1896) - Justified Jim Crow laws. "Separate but equal" was fine. [121]

Insular Cases (early 1900s) - Stated that Constitutional rights did not necessarily extend to US territories acquired during the Age of Imperialism. [84]

Muller v. Oregon (1908) - The Court ruled that women were not permitted to work such long hours because they might damage their bodies for maternity. [78]

Schenck v. US (1919) - Said that free speech was not absolute. One can't utter something that creates a "clear and present danger," as someone can't shout "FIRE!" in a crowded theater. [85]

Schechter Poultry Corp. v. US (1935) - Declared the New Deal's NIRA unconstitutional. [99]

US v. Butler (1936) - Declared the New Deal's AAA unconstitutional. [99]

Korematsu v. US (1944) - Japanese internment was constitutional, as in times of war, rights can be limited. [106]

Dennis v. US (1951) - Upheld the Smith Act during the Cold War which made it illegal to speak about overthrowing the government. Due process was limited because of a fear of communism. This was similar to the "clear and present danger" decision of the *Schenck* case. [112]

Brown v. Board of Education of Topeka, Kansas (1954) - Ended segregation in schools. "Separate but equal" is inherently unequal. [121]

Miranda v. Arizona (1966), ***Gideon v. Wainwright*** (1963), ***Mapp v. Ohio*** (1961) – All of these decisions of the Warren Court protected rights of the accused. [121]

Roe v. Wade, 1973 - Legalized abortion in 1973, but not in all cases. A woman's privacy was protected by the Ninth Amendment's reservation of rights for the people, the Fourth Amendment right of privacy, and the Fourteenth Amendment's protection of personal liberty.

Texas v. Johnson, 1989 - Burning of the American flag was protected by the First Amendment.

How do Checks and Balances Work?

	LEGISLATIVE	EXECUTIVE	JUDICIAL
LEGISLATIVE CHECKS		1. Can override vetoes by 2/3 vote 2. Senate can refuse to confirm a Presidential appointment	1. Can change the size of the Supreme Court
EXECUTIVE CHECKS	1. Can veto bills 2. Can call Congress into special session		1. Appoints Supreme Court justices 2. Grants pardons and reprieves
JUDICIAL CHECKS	1. Can declare an act of Congress to be unconstitutional (judicial review)	1. Can declare an act of the President to be unconstitutional	

Differences Between Thomas Jefferson and Alexander Hamilton

Issue	Thomas Jefferson	Alexander Hamilton
Who should have power in government?	The educated/ commoners	The propertied aristocracy
Give most power to the:	States	Federal or Central Gov't. (Strong Federal Gov't.)
Constitutional Interpretation	Strict — Don't give the Federal Government too much power to legislate	Loose — Allow the Federal Government to do whatever is "necessary and proper"
Stance on Army	Against! Gives government too much power	For! Will make the government powerful
National Bank	Con: Favors the rich	Pro: Stabilizes the economy
Favored foreign nation	France — They supported our revolution	England — the strongest nation; similar heritage
Preferred Economy	Agriculture	Industry and Commerce

These ideas would evolve into the first political parties.

How Did Our Two-Party System Develop?

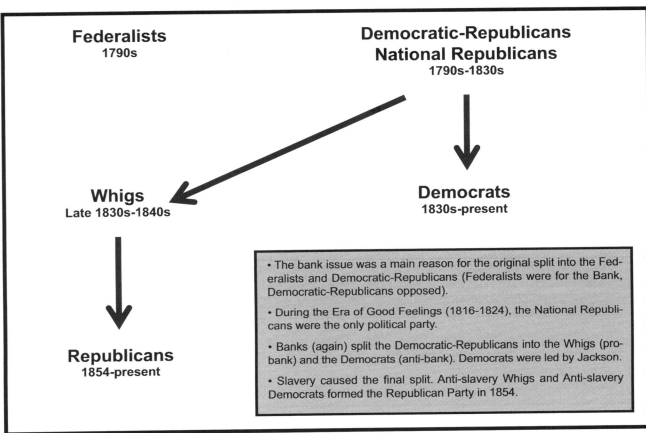

Federalists
1790s

Democratic-Republicans
National Republicans
1790s-1830s

Whigs
Late 1830s-1840s

Democrats
1830s-present

Republicans
1854-present

• The bank issue was a main reason for the original split into the Federalists and Democratic-Republicans (Federalists were for the Bank, Democratic-Republicans opposed).

• During the Era of Good Feelings (1816-1824), the National Republicans were the only political party.

• Banks (again) split the Democratic-Republicans into the Whigs (pro-bank) and the Democrats (anti-bank). Democrats were led by Jackson.

• Slavery caused the final split. Anti-slavery Whigs and Anti-slavery Democrats formed the Republican Party in 1854.

Look What the Jay Treaty with Britain Caused!

| Jay Treaty 1794 | → | XYZ Affair 1797 | → | Quasi War with France | → | Alien & Sedition Acts, 1798 | → | Virginia & Kentucky Resolutions 1798-99 |

A Quick Review of Tariffs

1. 1828 Tariff of Abominations raised rates, and nearly caused South Carolina to secede.

2. The Underwood Tariff of 1913 decreased rates after the Democrats took office.

3. The Smoot-Hawley Tariff of 1930 raised tariffs to the highest point since the Tariff of Abominations. This was done originally to protect the agriculture industry.

D ... **D**emocrats, Tariffs go **D**own, Help **D**ee poor, **D**eep or Solid South.

R ... **R**epublicans, **R**aise Tariffs, Less Taxes for the **R**ich, Favor **R**ailroads and **R**obber Barons.

Remember: When Democrats are in office, tariffs typically go down. When Republicans are in office, tariffs typically go up. Tariffs eased after World War II.

The Tariff of Abominations Led to...

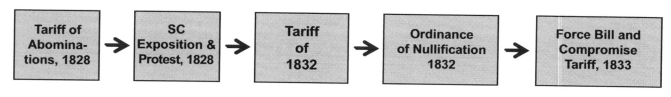

Tariff of Abominations, 1828 → SC Exposition & Protest, 1828 → Tariff of 1832 → Ordinance of Nullification 1832 → Force Bill and Compromise Tariff, 1833

Manifest Destiny

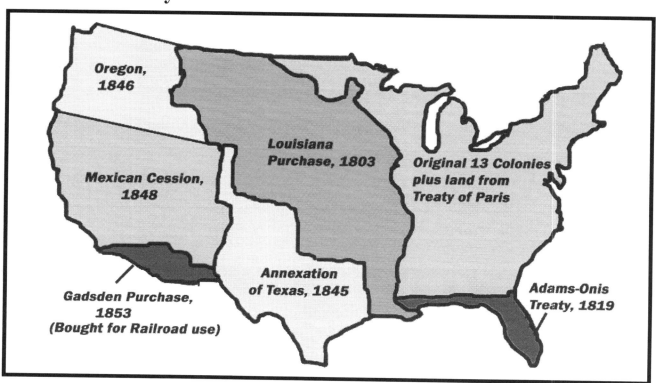

Oregon, 1846

Louisiana Purchase, 1803

Original 13 Colonies plus land from Treaty of Paris

Mexican Cession, 1848

Gadsden Purchase, 1853 (Bought for Railroad use)

Annexation of Texas, 1845

Adams-Onis Treaty, 1819

Slavery Compromises Prior to the Civil War *(Know these well!)*

Missouri Compromise of 1820 - Missouri was a slave state, no slavery north of the 36° 30' latitude line, Maine was a free state. It was brokered by Henry Clay.

Compromise of 1850 - Provided for: A Fugitive Slave Act, no slave trade in DC, the former Mexican Territory of Utah and New Mexico to have popular sovereignty, California to become a free state, Texas to give up western land and receive $10 million to pay off its debt. Authored by Henry Clay.

Kansas-Nebraska Act of 1854 - provided for popular sovereignty, or the right to choose if a state would have slavery or not. This led to *Bleeding Kansas*, and the *Lecompton Constitution* which approved slavery in Kansas. The compromise was authored by Stephen Douglas.

Slavery Legislation and Compromises, 1820-1854

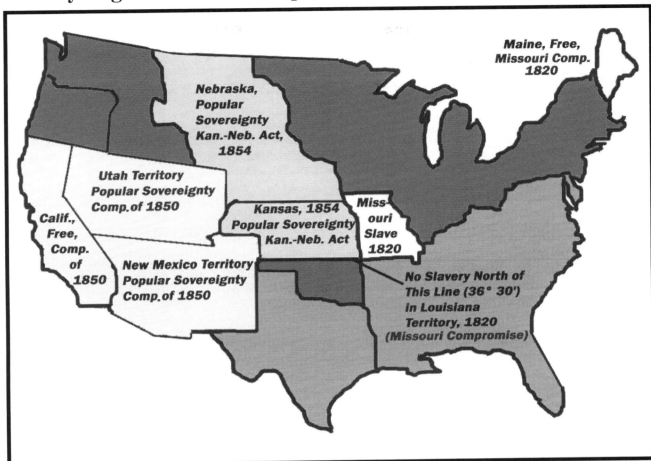

Differences Between the American Federation of Labor and the Knights of Labor

American Federal of Labor:
BAGS = **B**read Butter Issues / **A**FL / **G**ompers / **S**trike less with collective bargaining

Knights of Labor:
KUPS = **K**nights / **U**nskilled / **P**owderly / **S**trike more (Unskilled spellers can't spell cups)

Republican Policies, 1865-c1932

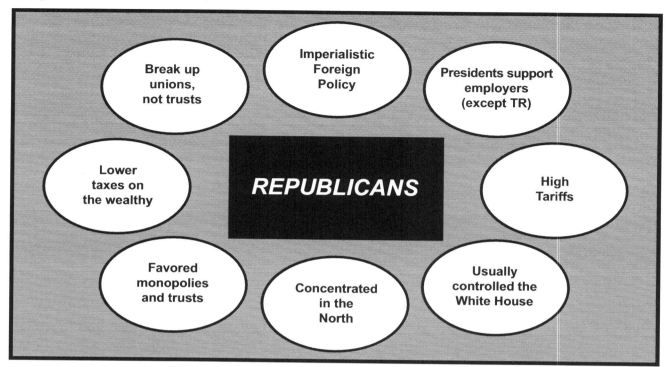

Democratic Policies, 1865-c1932

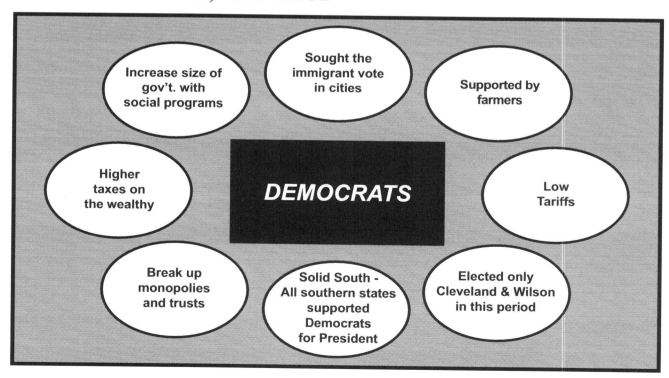

20th Century Presidential Programs and Slogans

Theodore Roosevelt (Rep): A *Square Deal* for Americans. He supported consumers over trusts. [76]

Woodrow Wilson (Dem); His *New Freedom* (defeated TR's **New Nationalism**) promised even more trustbusting. [77]

Warren G. Harding (Rep); Looked to *Return to Normalcy* after World War I. He died in office, and Calvin Coolidge was in office most of the 20s.

Franklin D. Roosevelt (Dem); *The New Deal* looked for public works, and hands-on government economic change. [97]

Harry Truman (Dem); *A Fair Deal* for social improvement, civil rights, and expanding education and healthcare. Remember, "Tru" was "Fair." [114-115]

Dwight Eisenhower (Rep); *Dynamic Conservatism*. The 1950s was a conservative time economically (government supported business), politically (McCarthyism), and socially (women were back at home). You should also know that Eisenhower signed the *Federal-Aid Highway Act in 1956*. This provided for the modern day **interstate highway system**.

John F. Kennedy (Dem); *The New Frontier* was a hope for solving poverty, racial prejudice, and providing international aid. [113]

Lyndon Johnson (Dem); *The Great Society* offered solutions for poverty, education, and an end to discrimination. [123]

Presidents 1965-Present

What you need to know!

Lyndon Johnson [123]

Richard Nixon [123-124]

Gerald Ford [124]

Jimmy Carter [125]

Ronald Reagan [125]

George H. W. Bush [125]

Bill Clinton [125-126]

George W. Bush [126]

Barack Obama [126]

Foreign Policy: Here's a Handy Time-Line

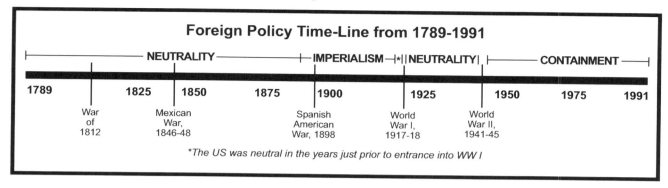

Foreign Policy Time-Line from 1789-1991

NEUTRALITY — IMPERIALISM — *| NEUTRALITY | — CONTAINMENT

1789   1825   1850   1875   1900   1925   1950   1975   1991

War of 1812

Mexican War, 1846-48

Spanish American War, 1898

World War I, 1917-18

World War II, 1941-45

*The US was neutral in the years just prior to entrance into WW I

Here are some people you may not know

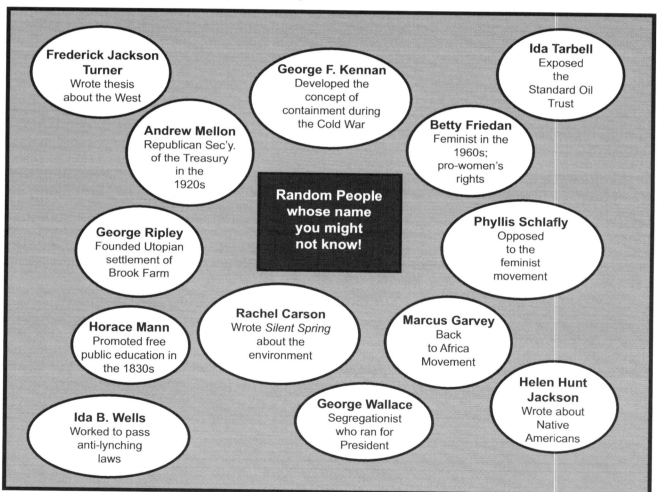

Frederick Jackson Turner
Wrote thesis about the West

George F. Kennan
Developed the concept of containment during the Cold War

Ida Tarbell
Exposed the Standard Oil Trust

Andrew Mellon
Republican Sec'y. of the Treasury in the 1920s

Betty Friedan
Feminist in the 1960s; pro-women's rights

Random People whose name you might not know!

George Ripley
Founded Utopian settlement of Brook Farm

Phyllis Schlafly
Opposed to the feminist movement

Horace Mann
Promoted free public education in the 1830s

Rachel Carson
Wrote *Silent Spring* about the environment

Marcus Garvey
Back to Africa Movement

Helen Hunt Jackson
Wrote about Native Americans

Ida B. Wells
Worked to pass anti-lynching laws

George Wallace
Segregationist who ran for President

13 Colonies Geography c1740

NORTH: Massachusetts, N. Hampshire, Connecticut, & Rhode Island
- Shipbuilding, Agriculture, Trade

MIDDLE: New York, Delaware, New Jersey, Pennsylvania
- Trade, Shipbuilding, Foodstuffs

SOUTH: Virginia and Maryland = Tobacco
North Carolina = Tobacco and Fur
South Carolina = Rice
Georgia = Rice and Indigo

Notes: